Escape To Africa

Henri Diamant

Escape To Africa

Henri Diamant

Apprentice House
Baltimore, Maryland

ISBN: 978-1-934074-68-8

Printed in the United States of America

First Edition

Cover photo by Harry Diamant
Book cover and internal design by Alexandra Attanasio, '12
Design editor: Mairead McKeron, '12

Published by Apprentice House
The Future of Publishing...Today!

Apprentice House
Communication Department
Loyola University Maryland
4501 N. Charles Street
Baltimore, MD 21210

410.617.5265
410.617.2198 (fax)
www.ApprenticeHouse.com
info@ApprenticeHouse.com

Map of Belgian Congo

1. Stanley Pool
2. Stanleyville
3. Livingstone Rapids
4. Leopoldville
5. Port Francqui
6. Luluabourg
7. Jadotville
8. Elisabethville
9. Lusambo

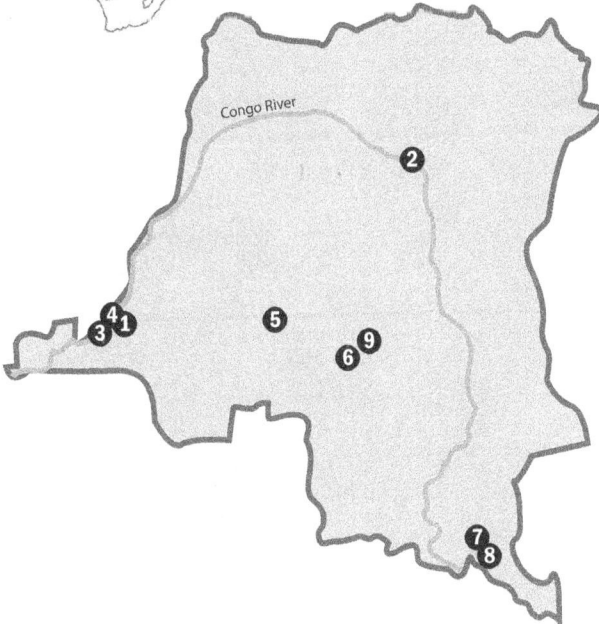

Table of Contents

Foreword ix
1. Congo, The Ultimate Destination 1
2. My Family 5
3. Mother's Family 11
4. My Father 15
5. The Wedding 19
6. Father's Career at Bata 27
7. Escape to Africa 43
8. First Glimpse of Africa 51
9. Lobito 55
10. Africa and the Congo 63
11. King Leopold II, David Livingstone & 77
     Henry Morton Stanley
12. Elisabethville, The End of Our Trip 87
13. Monsieur Rypar 91
14. Life in Elisabethville 109
15. My First Monkey 115
16. The Dark Days 123
17. Moving to Lusambo 127
18. Lusambo and the Sankuru River 133
19. Life in Lusambo 143
20. More About Life in the Bush 149
21. The Eventful Year of 1942 167
22. History of Leopoldville 173
23. Boarding School 179
24. New Bata Factory 183

25. Bimbo the Chimp 189
26. D-Day and the Move to Elisabethville 197
27. Tonsillitis and Cape Town 203
28. Becoming a Bata Man.............................211
29. Visiting America................................217
30. Back On the Job.................................223
31. Up in the Sky..................................229
32. My Transfer to America.........................237
33. First Months in America........................241
34. Life Interrupted 245
35. The Navy 253
36. Life of a Sailor 259
37. The Missing Salem 265
38. Our Wedding...................................271
Acknowledgments..................................275
Glossary 276
Epilogue..277

Foreword

The decision to write this memoir was motivated by
several factors, two of which were truly vital and should be
mentioned here.

The first one came by way of our daughter Michele. Her
interest in family roots, and her intense curiosity about my
years in Africa, became the most compelling arguments for
this work.

The second is linked to our 2005 European trip. My
wife Leila and I went there for a reunion of cousins (on
Grandma's Soffer side of the family) near Vienna, Austria,
and for a visit to the Czech Republic. During the reunion,
I heard more about the Diamant/Soffer history than I had
ever been exposed to before. And that made me realize that
I needed to leave some kind of legacy for posterity. By the
way, our reunion might as well have been held at the UN,
considering all the various languages that were used between
us; Czech, German, Yiddish, Hebrew and English. Spanish
and French were not represented because cousins from
Chile and France could not make it to Austria.

I should also mention that the journey through
the Czech Republic became, quite unexpectedly, an
unquestionable emotional experience. I was much surprised
at the depth of my feelings when, after almost 70 years, I

saw once again our Grandparents' homes in Kravsko and Lostice. That clinched it, and I started writing the minute I returned home.

1. Congo, The Ultimate Destination

I was eight years old in 1938 when our parents told us, my older brother Harry and me, that we were going to leave our home in Brno (Czechoslovakia at the time, Czech Republic today) and move to some country called Romania. I had never heard of Romania, and could not grasp why we were suddenly leaving our relatives and friends, and moving far away from home. But several weeks later I overheard our parents deliberating about lost passports, a missed opportunity in Romania and father's acceptance of a position in Africa. Now that really made me sit up and take notice. All I had to hear was the name of that mysterious and thrilling continent and, just like that, my reluctance to leave friends and family vanished in a flash. And, while I will give further on more details about the strange set of circumstances that led us to Africa, I think it appropriate to disclose right now the thoughts that popped into my young mind the minute I heard about our impending move to the "Dark Continent".

Mystifying AFRICA...Wow, and triple wow, I just could not believe that I was destined to live on the African Continent. How lucky can a guy get. After all, that mysterious continent was synonymous with adventure, pygmies, jungles and pets. And not just any pets, but the exotic, fascinating and wonderful pets of the Rain Forest.

The proof of all this could be readily seen in every Tarzan movie that was ever made. Just think of that everlasting bond between Tarzan and Cheetah. For me, a kid who always fantasized about animals, travel, and adventure in exotic lands, this was the ultimate prospect of things to come, of dreams merging into reality. And so, I started at once to collect silver foil candy wrappers, since I knew for a fact that this was by far the top currency in Africa (I read all about it in one of my adventure books). And although I could not even guess as to how much foil was required to get a couple of chimps, I felt deep down that it had to be quite a lot. Wonderful pets like chimps and monkeys do not come cheap. But as I pondered about all this, I suddenly had two contrasting thoughts. The first one was quite tempting because it urged me to consume large quantities of candies in order to accumulate a good hoard of those precious foil wrappers. But the flip side hinted that over-eating candies usually brought on the misery of indigestion. However, in the scheme of things, this was a small "sacrifice" to pay and I quickly put my plan into action, just like any other eight year old boy would have done under the same circumstances. By the way, my name is Henri, or Jindrich in Czech.

My very active imagination started to work overtime when I learned that we were actually on our way to the Belgian Congo, a country deep in the very heart of Africa. It is now the Democratic Republic of the Congo, but it had two prior names in the recent past. At independence, in that momentous year of 1960, it was The Republic of the Congo. But in 1971, for the sake of something called "National

Authenticity", President Joseph Desire Mobutu, changed
it to the "Republic of Zaire" (which is, the native name for
the Congo River). He also replaced some of the colonial-
era names; Leopoldville, the capital, became Kinshasa,
Elisabethville became Lubumbashi, etc (I will be using the
colonial-era names, but the current names will appear in
a comparison chart at the end of this memoir). He even
altered his own title to "President Mobutu Sese Seko Kuku
Ngwendu Wa Za Banga ", a title that did not bode well for
the future. It translates as "The all-powerful Warlord who,
because of his endurance and inflexible will to win, will go
from conquest to conquest, leaving fire in his wake". In the
end, his dictatorship brought only death, misery and poverty
to a country that should have had a bright destiny.

In 1973, Mobutu took other steps. He nationalized many
of the large enterprises owned by European Expatriates,
and arranged for Zairien managers to take full control of
these companies. He did all this, the name changes and the
nationalization of large properties, in a desperate attempt
to unify a country with no sense of nationhood, a country
that was still divided by strong tribal allegiances. Prior to
European encroachments, nationhood was an unknown
concept, and it did not help, when Congo was carved
out of south central Africa in the late eighteen hundreds,
that no consideration was given to social, ethnic, or tribal
boundaries. By the way, this particular region, largely
unexplored until the early 1900's, was eventually found to be
an inhospitable place with an extremely unhealthy climate
and deadly tropical diseases.Plus, if that wasn't enough

to keep you away, there were many vivid reports about cannibalism and other gruesome customs. However, there were also persistent rumors of vast mineral deposits, and that was what eventually shaped Europe's thrust into Africa.

I was too young to give any thoughts to potential dangers, but my parents must have been fully aware of them. Yet they had the courage to take their young sons and move to this forbidding land where even the language loomed as a large obstacle to them. The official language in the Congo was, and still is, French...a language my parents did not understand at all.

Later on, as I grew older, it became clear that our parents' concern about the threatening situation in Germany, and their deep sense of foreboding about the future of Czechoslovakia, made them persevere in their resolve to leave Europe, even if it meant moving to that unknown and dangerous country in Africa. I will forever remain grateful to them for doing this, despite all the appeals and arguments that the rest of the family used to make them change their minds.As a result we lived to see Hitler's defeat, while most of our relatives perished in the Holocaust.

2. My Family

Now, I will switch gears and go back to where I should have begun this memoir. In other words, I will write about our dear parents, Julius and Amalie Diamant. Not only were they the foundation of our family but, as I mentioned earlier, thanks to their extraordinary courage and foresight, they saved us from the horrors of the Holocaust. And they also succeeded, despite challenging circumstances, to offer us an extraordinary life in the tropics. A life of opportunities and challenges that actually prepared Harry and me for almost anything the future had in store for us.

Both of our parents hailed from Moravia, an area of central Europe that, until 1918, was part of the Austro-Hungarian Empire. After the First World War it became part of the newly formed Republic of Czechoslovakia. Now, of course, it is called the Czech Republic because the Province of Slovakia opted out the federation, and became the Slovak Republic.

Father was born on December 31st, 1900, in the Moravian village of Kravsco.

Kravsko, some six miles from the town of Znojmo, is typical of the other villages in the area, an area of vast forests and fertile fields. The houses have thick stucco walls, small windows and red-tiled roofs. The streets are narrow and wind in a random way between the small homes. Our grandparents' property stood close to a charming bridge, right next to a pond fed by a meandering river. grandpa Joseph and grandma Ernestine owned the village's general store and, according to all indications, lead a decent life. They had four children; our father Julius, Uncle Arnold, Aunt Louisa and the oldest, Aunt Johanna. Theirs was the only Jewish family in the village.

The general store was on the right side of the property, with its front window and entrance facing a small parking area right off the street. Next came the living quarters, a storage room, stables for horses and, on the left side of the courtyard, a rental property that provided a good income for our grandparents. The well, with a hand pump, stood outside the kitchen door, while the outhouse was stuck all the way in the back of the yard.

I remember the time when, swollen by unusually heavy rains, the pond rose high enough to flood the courtyard and make life thoroughly miserable for our grandparents. But they were rewarded for their troubles with a good supply of fresh fish when swiftly receding waters trapped a bunch of them in the courtyard.

I also remember that Grandma force-fed geese so they would produce more fat and grow enlarged livers. This process is not very complicated, and still used to this day throughout the World, even though it does not look very humane. The animal is kept inactive in a narrow cage and, several times a day, a funnel is inserted down its throat so that food can be forced into the belly with the help

of a wooden dowel. By the way, goose fat made excellent
sandwiches. The best ones were made with thick slices of a
farmer's dark bread, liberal amounts of goose fat generously
seasoned with pepper and salt, and a mountain of delicious
cold cuts. Hello clogged arteries...

Two of the major crops grown around Kravsko were
cucumbers and cabbage. They were used in large part
to make pickles and sauerkraut, both of them in great
demand all over the country. As a matter of fact, that
general area was actually known as the pickle district of
Moravia. Fermentation was made in wooden barrels, and
farmers always kept a few of them on hand for year-round
consumption.

Fruit trees were plentiful. Even country roads were
lined with them. And these particular trees, as well as some
in private orchards, were leased to individuals for the whole
summer, a custom that is still practiced today. Just think
about it, one could be living in a large town and yet have
the thrill of harvesting cherries, or some other fruit, right
from one's "own" tree during an entire summer season. And
while it is true that many of our orchards let you " pick
your own ", it is not really the same thing since it does not
involve leasing a tree for a whole summer season. Anyway,
our grandfather used to lease several fruit trees every season,
and we had great fun picking the juicy fruits whenever we
came to Kravsko. I used to stuff myself silly with cherries;
my very favorite fruit. And, staying on the subject of gorging
oneself, I recall that Harry and I were unable to keep our
fingers out of the big barrels that contained grandpa's

delicious pickles. We usually chose the largest ones, washed off the brine and went to work. What a delicacy that was, as were the wild strawberries and mushrooms that we picked during our hikes through the forest. Grandma's mushroom soups and gravies were to die for. Of course, grandpa knew the difference between edible and poisonous mushrooms, but if one could not differentiate between them, the way to play it safe was to have a pharmacist check them over (they did this free of charge). Mushrooms were also dried for winter cooking. They were cleaned, and left to dry on sunny kitchen window-sills. This concentrated the flavor and greatly enhanced the mushrooms' unique taste in every dish they were used for.

I must not forget to mention Kravsko's prominent "Castle", built by an Italian Count in the late 1700's. The local people refer to it as a castle, but it really does not look like one since it does not have turrets, or even a moat. It is a manor house, in the renaissance style of Italy's Palazzi, which were the summer residences of wealthy Italians. The symmetrical facade is three stories high and has a different architectural treatment on each level. The sweeping gravel driveway and the fountain on the front lawn heighten the elegance of the property. The last Italian owner used it for his summer residence through 1939. Hunting was his favorite hobby, and he spent much time riding through the deep forest and large fields that were part of the estate. Father told me that the fresh game was hung in the cellar, and left to age for a very long time. Apparently, this aging process went on for so long that the game turned rather "ripe" by the time it was cooked.

I also remember my father's favorite joke about a neighboring village known for its weekly "farmers' market day" that was held on Thursdays. It became so successful that the villagers decided to petition the mayor for a second market day, and formed a small group that went to discuss the matter with him. Unfortunately, in all the excitement, the delegation mistakenly asked for two "Thursdays" per week... From then on, any outsider visiting the village and cracking a joke about two Thursdays a week, ran the real danger of bodily harm and a quick expulsion from the village.

As a final note about Kravsko, I feel compelled to report about what happened to the members of our family.

Grandpa passed away in 1938, and was buried in Znojmo's Jewish cemetery. Unfortunately, this cemetery was desecrated during the Nazi occupation and its gravestones were used to pave city streets. The location of the grave was lost forever.

Grandma was deported and perished in 1942 in the Teresienstadt Concentration Camp.

Aunt Johanna (Father's oldest sibling, born in 1896) married Uncle Paul Katz and gave birth to two daughters, Susanne and Ruth. They lived in Vienna until 1938, when they managed to immigrate to the USA.

Aunt Louise (Father's other sister, born in 1897) was deported with her husband Kurt Reich and sons Heinz, Morritz and Bertholt. They all perished in the Lublin concentration camp in 1942. They got to Lublin via Terezin.

Uncle Arnold (Father's brother, born in 1899) was deported with his wife Emmy and sons Tommy and Josef. His wife and children were gassed when the family reached Auschwitz, via Terezin, in 1942. Incredibly, Uncle Arnold managed to survive the horrors of the camp and the "death march" that the Nazis organized in a futile attempt to hide the inmates from the onrushing Allied Forces. He was liberated, and eventually made it to the States. It took some time, but eventually he regained his health, married a lovely lady by the name of Dora, and lived out his life on a chicken farm in Vineland, New Jersey.

3. Mother's Family

Our Mother was born in the town of Lostice, Moravia, on July 6, 1906, to Elise and Karl Hirsch. Like all towns and cities in that part of Europe, Lostice evolved around the proverbial town square that is paved over with cobblestones, and is surrounded by homes, the ever present church, several shops and a couple of taverns. The urban area dates back many centuries. I saw documents in the United States Holocaust Memorial Museum in Washington, D.C. that mention a Jewish presence in town from the early 1500's. Jews lived all over town, without any apparent restrictions or discrimination, until 1727. Later, the Austrian Emperor decided that Jews should not live in the vicinity of a church, and the town council was forced to relocate the entire Jewish population within a single neighborhood, thus creating, essentially, a ghetto. The last synagogue, a rather plain structure, was built in the early 1800 s. It is currently under the care of the township because a new Jewish Community Association could not be formed after World War II (the final records of the old Jewish Community Association are dated 1940, the year that it was abolished by the Nazis)... Only 11 survivors came back after the war, out of some 50 deportees. Unfortunately, none were from our family.

Grandfather was a butcher. He was a large man well

over six feet tall, with broad shoulders, large back and a thick neck. He was so tall that he had to hunch down to get through doorways.

I remember most vividly (I guess because of my love of animals) that he used a dogcart, pulled by two beautiful Saint Bernards, to transport batches of meat between the farm and his downtown butcher shop. Those dogs were as gentle as they were big, and we loved playing with them. I particularly liked riding them horseback fashion (whenever they let me), and playing cowboys (I never did master a lasso). Yes, they were gentle with us, but no stranger ever dared enter the yard without Grandfather's permission.

Our grandparents did not raise cattle or cultivate fields, but the large farmyard was always full of chickens, ducks and geese, and many fruit trees grew in the back. The house, barns and other structures were clustered around the yard in a random way. At the front of the farm was a wide gate that extended from the house to the barn at the opposite side of the property. A regular-size door was cut into its right side, so that one could walk through without opening the entire gate. The house had thick walls, low ceilings with exposed wooden beams and small windows. As expected, an outhouse was located at the back of the yard, and a well with a hand pump sat next to the side of the house.

The setting of the farm was quite unique, because of a narrow canal that ran between one side of the property and the street. It was built to carry water from the river to a nearby mill, and we had to cross over a small pedestrian bridge whenever we wanted to get to the street. We could have used the dirt road on the opposite side of the farm, but that would have taken us the long way around (livestock was brought to the farm by that road). However, it was the close proximity to the river that made the surroundings so kid-friendly. This river was right around the bend of the road, and the water was visible from the back of the farmyard. We fished there whenever we came for our infrequent visits, but we rarely caught anything worth the trouble.

Grandpa used one of the outbuildings to butcher the livestock and to carry out other aspects of his trade. His sausages were the greatest ever, especially when eaten right out of the kettle. Yes, he was quite a butcher, but one with an unfortunate dietary problem. He consumed large quantities of meat three times a day, morning, noon and evening, with hardly ever anything else. Inevitably this caught up with him. He became ill and went to see a doctor who told him, in no uncertain terms, that he had to overcome his meat addiction and start eating vegetables, fruits, etc. However as expected, that did not last long. Mother told me that he tried very hard to follow the doctor's instructions, but he just could not force himself to do it. So, he decided that he would "rather die a happy man, than lead an unhappy life", and went right back to his old ways. In the end, it was not his wrong eating habit that did him in, it was a Nazi concentration camp.

I am unable to say much about Grandma Elise because I did not get to know her. She died when mother was just a little girl.

Grandma Elise had two sisters, and both aunts became prominent in mother's life after her mother passed away.

Aunt Helena married Edvard Schwarzbart, and moved to Brno where her new husband practiced veterinary medicine.

Aunt Irma married our Grandfather and became mother's step mother. In due time, they had two daughters, our mother's half sisters Lyzi and Greta.

I do not know exactly what happened after Grandfather remarried, except that mother left her home and moved to Brno. The only thing she ever mentioned to us was to say that Aunt Helena and Uncle Edvard raised her as their own daughter and that Brno became her new hometown. She remained with them until she married Father.

Tragically, each person mentioned in this chapter, except of course mother, was deported and perished in a concentration camp. They were all rounded up in 1942, and sent to Treblinky via Terezin.

4. My Father

Father, together with his brother and sisters, attended a public school in Znojmo, They lived in town all week long, and came home only weekends because grandpa's horse and buggy couldn't possibly make the trip each day. They either lived with some relatives in Znojmo, or were placed in a private boardinghouse. I do not know which.

It was during the dismal year of 1914 that father graduated from high school, just as Europe was thrust into World War I. Then, when the time came to conscript all men born in 1900, father was mobilized by the Austrian military. However, had he been born but a few hours later, I believe that he would have missed the draft altogether and would have never fought in the war. These few hours would have shifted his name from the list of 1900 (remember that he was born December 31, 1900), over to the subsequent list of 1901, the year that should have escaped the draft because the war was winding down at that time. As it was, father reported to the army in the early part of 1917 and, after a brief period of basic training, found himself with the Austrian Expeditionary Force fighting on the Italian front.

Ultimately, the War that was to end all Wars ran its sad course, and a treaty was signed in the Hall of Mirrors, inside the Palace of Versailles, on the outskirts of Paris. The signing took place on November 11, 1918.

The birth of Czechoslovakia was one of the upshots of Austria's defeat. The new nation united the provinces of Moravia, Bohemia and Slovakia, and its young government immediately embarked on molding the republic into one of the most liberal and progressive countries of Europe.

But the country also required the formation of a national army, and the republic lost no time drafting its young men into military service. And guess who was drafted for a second time in his young life? Father eventually graduated into a full-fledged dragoon (a heavily armed cavalryman), and spent two years in the Czech army before reverting to civilian life at the end of 1922.

Although I have only faint memories of father's accounts of his years in the Czech army, I recall distinctly his comments about the horses that were used by the cavalry. Evidently some of them were conscripted, just like the men, and at times their previous lives came to haunt inexperienced riders during basic training. Most troublesome were the horses that had worked on daily delivery routes, such as milk runs. They were conditioned to stop on their own, without any prodding, in front of customers' houses, and remain standing in place until the produce was taken to the front door and the driver came back to the wagon. Apparently, there were times when the man fell asleep, and it was left up to the horse to stop and wait patiently until his master delivered the goods. Problems arose when a new regiment went on field trips, and rode through a town known by one of these horses. The animal, still unfamiliar with military life, responded to his original training, and did what he was taught to do, he stopped dead in his tracks whenever he came across a familiar house. Of course, he refused to budge until his rider dismounted, went to the door and climbed back in the saddle. Think how humiliating and disconcerting that must have been for the unseasoned dragoon.

5. The Wedding

Following his graduation from high school, father obtained an apprenticeship at a dry-goods retail store in Znojmo. It was then that he realized how much he liked the retail business, and that he was going to make it his life's career. He left the apprenticeship only because he was drafted into the Austrian army.

After his discharge, he returned home where he helped to run the family business, and gradually put on some weight on his mother's renowned cooking (in light of the awful food that he ate in the army, his mother's cooking was pure bliss). However, this utopia was short-lived because, as mentioned earlier, he was drafted a second time. He served in the Czech army until 1922.

After his discharge, Father decided to pursue his luck in a large city. And the one that was reasonably close, and happened to be especially attractive to him was, of course, the famous city of Vienna. But what really helped him decide on Vienna, was the fact that his sister Johanna, her husband Paul Katz and their first child, daughter Susanne, were already living there. No other city offered all these advantages, and father made his move without reservations (Johanna's cooking was second best only to their mother's).

Once in Vienna, it did not take long before he landed a retail position. He became a salesman in a shoe store on Favoriten Strasse, owned, interestingly enough, by a Rudolf Diamant. This man was not related to our family, but father's last name may have helped him get his "shoe" in the door (after all, we are talking about a shoe store, not a foot store). Right from the start, father truly enjoyed his job, and he worked hard on mastering all the fine points of the retail business.

The result of this zeal was that father quickly became an accomplished salesman who bolstered the store's proceeds. He ended up working for Rudolf Diamant from 1922 until 1928.

During the course of these years something momentous happened. Something quite wonderful actually. Father married mother.

Now, one must wonder how a man living in Vienna could meet, court and marry a young woman in Brno. Especially since all this went on when long trips were difficult to undertake and rather expensive on a salesman's salary. Another problem was the lack of easy and affordable communications.

But love conquers all, and father did not let such mundane issues stop him from courting mother.

Initially they met at a wedding in Znojmo. I do not know exactly who was getting hitched, but I do know that it was some one from the Schwarzbart side of the family (grandma Ernestine's sister was married to Bernard Schwartzbart). As luck would have it, the Schwarzbarts from Brno came to the happy event, and mother tagged along with them.

Weddings in those days were not the elaborate affairs that are the norm today. For the most part, out of town guests usually stayed with relatives , even if it meant that some of them had to spend a couple of nights on the floor. Of course, that small detail never stopped any one from having a great time at a wedding.

Father did not relish using the floor for a couple of nights, and so he did his best to find a good substitute the minute he came in. And find one he did. It was a small couch that was set apart from the main area of the living room, in a corner that actually offered some privacy. But, as he was about ready to enjoy a peaceful night, he noticed, across the crowded room, a very attractive young woman struggling to get comfortable on the bare floor.Not surprisingly, before he even realized what was happening, he walked over and gallantly offered his private couch to the enchanting woman. That was Amalie, our future mother.

I understand that father did not get much rest that night, and it was not due merely to the hardness of the floor. Father could not stop thinking about the beautiful Amalie. It was love at first sight.

Early the following morning, they met for breakfast, and wound up spending the whole day together. They quickly developed a deep fondness for each other, and promised to keep in touch after they parted and returned to their respective homes.

There is no doubt whatsoever that they kept their promises, and that father became very good at keeping alive a "long distance" courtship. They were married hardly a year after they met. The wedding took place in 1926, at the Schwarzbart's home in Brno.

The newly-wed couple found a small apartment in Vienna and while father resumed his work at the shoe store, mother spent long hours visiting with her brand new sister-in-law Johanna. In fact, she desperately needed to acquire quickly some fundamental knowledge about cooking meals. She was good at many things, but cooking was not one of them. Her aunt and uncle, with no children of their own, had pampered mother in the pure sense of the word and, although she learned to play the piano and enjoy operas, she acquired very little experience in running a household, and even less preparing meals.

On the other hand, Johanna was definitely an experienced homemaker and, like Grandma Ernestine, a great cook. In the end, mother learned enough from Johanna to manage on her own, and to stop relying on the neighborhood restaurant to keep father from going hungry. Still, it must be noted that in true fashion of newly-wed husbands, father never complained about their meals, not even when some of them happened to get scorched. Mother had the unfortunate habit of forgetting about the oven whenever she played the piano.

Mother fell in love with lively Vienna, the Paris of the South, a Vienna that was the home of the waltz and the operetta. The city that had been, at one time or another, the home of such famous composers as Joseph Haydn, Wolfgang Amadeus Mozart, Ludwig van Beethoven, Johann

Strauss and many others. It was a city full of joie-de-vivre and culture, with many museums, beautiful parks, imposing palaces and, of course, the celebrated Danube River. Father and mother made the most of what the city had to offer, the theaters, movie houses and the neighborhood coffeehouses where they whiled away many pleasant evenings with family and friends. Then there was the Prater, Vienna's large amusement park with its celebrated Ferris wheel. And because father was wild about horses, they frequently went to see the graceful white Lippizan stallions of the prestigious Spanish Riding School. Father was entranced by the "Haute Ecole" riding maneuvers and the intricate routines flawlessly executed by these magnificent animals. To this day, the most famous drill is the "Capriole", in which the horse leaps into the air while kicking its rear legs backward. The Lippizans, which are one of Austria's major cultural heritages, are the direct descendents of the oldest classic horse breed in Europe. Its origin dates from the 1500s when Archduke Karl II, the son of Emperor Ferdinand I, founded a stud farm in the village of Lipizza, hence the name Lipizzan Horses (also known as Lipizzaner). These horses are born black, but most of them turn entirely white within about a year. Only white stallions are featured in the performances of the Spanish Riding School. By the way, had it not been for the efforts of General George Patton, the school and its horses would have been annihilated during World War II. What a great tragedy that would have been.

The little village of Piber, approximately 35 km west of Gratz, in the beautiful countryside of Austria's west Styria, is the home of these exquisite Lipizzan horses. Fortunately, Leila and I were able to see them there when we visited Europe in 2005. It took us most of the day to go through the immense complex, which includes a museum full of carefully restored antique horse carriages. We got great pleasure from the graceful white mares and cute black foals. Their barn was immaculate; with not the slightest hint of manure in the air. We later learned that all the barns on the grounds were cleaned every two hours, around the clock.

Getting back to the 1920s, I should add that mother's first cousin Steffy, her husband Hugo Gratzer and son Otto also lived in Vienna during that period. Hugo was an auto mechanic and Steffy a seamstress. The fact that mother had a relative from her own side of the family at hand, made her life in Vienna that much more delightful. Years later, we found that Steffy, and her family, were the only ones on mother's side who escaped with their lives. They had left Vienna when Jews were still allowed to travel, and had booked passage on a ship bound for the U.S.A. But when they reached New York, none of the passengers were permitted to disembark, and the ship was ordered to return to Germany. The captain, a German mind you, did not want to be part of such cruelty and, instead, sailed into Cuba. Once again, the ship was turned away with all its unfortunate passengers. So, he tried again, and went to Caracas, in Venezuela. Bingo, that worked and the Grazers were given a new lease on life. They became a prominent family in Caracas.

Anyway, it was during our parents' happy days in Vienna that Harry appeared on the scene. He was born on February 22, 1928. And a few months later, another notable event unfolded.

Father found out about a great business opportunity that fit perfectly into his long-term plans. An established shoe store had come on the market in the capital city of Berlin, Germany. And, what made this potential acquisition especially interesting, was the financial clause. The terms required only a minimal amount of up-front financing, an amount that was within the range of father's affordability. Obviously, this was the break that father had been praying for, and he wasted little time closing the deal.

The family moved to Berlin at the end of 1928, and began a new kind of life, the life of a proprietor of a small retail shop. A life that turned out to be full of hard work, long hours and nagging financial worries. Father and mother worked side-by- side in the store, and spent little time on social activities.

Father changed the store's name to "Schuh Haus Diamant", and immediately turned his efforts toward improving profitability and sales. He reduced expenses by carefully managing the level of the inventory, and improved sales by replacing the store's limited assortment of styles with more alluring and catchy patterns and colors.

As luck would have it, father decided early on to stock the store with merchandise produced by a well-known Czech manufacturer, the Bata Shoe Company. In the footwear industry, the Bata Shoe Company was renowned for the high quality of its production and for its mid-priced fashionable footwear. In addition, the company had ongoing programs for cooperative advertising campaigns and a guaranteed 24-hour re-supply policy. Obviously, that was exactly what father needed for his new store, and he made good use of all the advantages that came with the Bata brand.

Over the months, father developed a personal relationship with some of the Bata's marketing managers, and it did not take long before they tried to recruit him for the company. They recognized his talents and decided that he would be a great asset for the firm. Bata was expanding rapidly, and it was in need of capable men and women, especially those with some years of retail experience.

It was around that time that a great event occurred-my birth. I was born on March 24, 1930, and a few months later, father signed up with Bata's retail division in Czechoslovakia.

We left Berlin during the month of November 1930.

6. Father's Career At Bata

I do not know why father abandoned his dream of
owning and running his own store. Maybe it was on account
of me. I was another mouth to feed and the growing family
needed a decent and dependable income, the kind that
one could not really expect from a small retail business.
The company he was joining was known for great career
opportunities, above average pay and exceptional benefits,
such as the company-managed savings accounts that
rewarded employees with the unheard of yearly yield of ten
percent.

Without question, future events proved that father
made the right decision to join the Bata organization.
And, since he often spoke of those times, I was left with a
good appreciation of what the company was all about, the
company that eventually affected our lives to such a great
degree.

The founder of the company, Mr. Thomas Bata, became
an apprentice in his father's modest footwear-manufacturing
establishment during the late 1800s. By 1932, the year that
he died in the crash of the company-owned airplane, he had
transformed his hometown of Zlin, Czechoslovakia, into a
modern industrial center that mass-produced some thirty-
six million pairs of footwear per year. The town, about 150

miles east of Prague, was owned entirely by the company, and employed a total of 20,000 workers. It featured low-rent housing, free access to medical care, schools, a cinema, a great indoor market, a department store, and large athletic facilities where various company teams competed vigorously for trophies. It became a global enterprise, with an industrial center famous for its mass production techniques and up-to-date technology. It was the most modern enterprise in the country, wielding a huge economic impact on the young republic and, to some extent, the world across state borders. For instance, there was the time when the German railroads, which moved the bulk of Zlin's exports to various German seaports (the Czech Republic being a land-locked country), informed the company about a substantial freight-rate increase. The company did not even bother to acknowledge receipt of the new rates, much less enter into any negotiations about them. Instead, it purchased a large fleet of trucks and started to do its own hauling across Germany. Within a few weeks, according to father, the railroads canceled the new freight rates, submitted some of the lowest rates ever, and took those dreadful trucks off the company's hands by purchasing them at premium prices.

Father also mentioned a couple of other instances that I found really interesting. The first one had to do with the extraordinary concept (we must remember that we are talking about the1930s) that went into the making of the chairman's office in the company's new headquarters building. The architects installed it in an elevator that moved swiftly and quietly up and down the 16 floors of the headquarters. This saved the chairman's time and kept the office personnel on its toes... no one knew when the boss would pop-up unannounced on their floor. By the way, the boss at that time was Jan Bata, he took over the management of the company after Thomas' death. They were stepbrothers, and Jan remained in charge until Thomas Junior came of age.

The other instance tells of Bata's entry into Africa. The initial decision to break into that market was made in the early 1930s, when the company charged two budding marketing managers to size up the business outlook on the continent. One was instructed to do his research up and down the East Coast, while the other was assigned to the West Coast. The one that had gone to the East Coast telexed the following discouraging news; "No one is wearing any footwear. No reason to waste time. Returning home". Then headquarters received the now-famous telex from the second guy: "See great opportunity. Everyone here in need of their very first pair of shoes". It is not difficult to guess which one of them was promoted quickly to a high management position in the expanding export division.

At any rate, once father made the move, he charged aggressively into his new job and, thanks to his prior experience in the retail business, easily impressed management during initial evaluation, and over the tough training period in Zlin. As a result, it did not take long before he was placed in charge of one of the low-volume shoe stores that were the training grounds for upcoming retail managers.

This store was located in the small town of Slavkov, a short distance from Brno, the second largest city in Czechoslovakia and the capital of the province of Moravia. And while it was a small town according to its size, it really was a giant by historical dimensions. History refers to it by the German name of Austerlitz, the place where a famous battle of the Napoleonic wars was fought on December 2, 1805. During that engagement, Napoleon's small expeditionary force completely crushed the much larger army that had been hurled against it by a coalition of the Austrian and Russian military forces.

Outside of Slavkov, at a junction of the road leading to the highway that connects the cities of Brno and Olomouc, one can still have a meal at the Stara Posta Inn, the very same tavern that Napoleon used during the night of that famous December day, in 1805. The next morning, he went to Presburg to sign the Peace Treaty that forced Austria to relinquish Venice and the Tyrol, and paved the way for Napoleon to become the master of Central Europe. His reign ended in 1815, when he met his final defeat at the bloody battle of Waterloo, a small Belgian village some 10 miles southeast of Brussels. He was exiled to the island of Saint Helena, where he died of cancer in 1821. Napoleon Bonaparte's body is buried in Paris, beneath the dome of the Hotel des Invalides, a hospital for sick and aged soldiers.

In 1933 father took over a large store in Sumperk, in the vicinity of the city of Olomouc. This promotion came with a substantial pay increase, an increase that motivated father to purchase the family's first car. Having a car in those days was rather exceptional, and the fact that father could afford one was clear indication that, true to its reputation, the company never failed to link pay to performance and hard work.

Another noteworthy event happened that year. Harry started his formal education and entered first grade. How fitting that he reached this milestone in the proximity of Olomouc, a well-known college town.

Father's new responsibility did not overwhelm him for a moment, and he proved again that he could be trusted to handle effectively and proficiently any task that was assigned to him. And so, a couple of years later, he was promoted to District Manager of the Znojmo region. As a result, we had to move once again. But this time no one complained because we were moving closer to Kravsko and our grandparents.

As District Manager, father had two distinct areas of responsibilities. He had to manage the largest store in his District, the one located in the center of Znojmo, and at the same time supervise all the units in surrounding towns.

The large store faced Horni Zamesti, Znojmo's major square. It was the only modern structure around the square, and with its four floors it was also one of the tallest. It had a flat roof and a large BATA sign prominently displayed at the very top of the building.

The entire first floor, bright and attractively appointed, was devoted to retail sales. It featured comfortable chairs, large displays and a concealed warehouse full of merchandise. The second floor held a large shoe-repair workshop on one side, and several pedicure booths on the other.

The third floor was reserved for single employees. It had several dorms and a large area for dining and social activities. The manager's apartment occupied the complete fourth floor.

Our family had a maid because mother worked with father on the sales floor. She supervised the cash registers, and kept an eye on the entire business during father's frequent trips into the district. The maid took care of us kids, cleaned the apartment and did some cooking. Occasionally, we were allowed to play with the toys displayed in the children's section of the store (the company manufactured amazing toys, most of them molded in rubber). I spent long and happy hours in the company of all kinds of handsomely detailed toy soldiers and military hardware. The array included horse-drawn guns that were capable of firing rubber shells. And those shells easily toppled enemy troops, even at some distance (provided I aimed well, which was not always easy to do).Several of the soldiers held little electric bulbs that flashed Morse codes when activated by remote control. Let me assure you, I had great fun with all that military hardware.

I can truly say that we were good kids, and usually managed to stay out of serious trouble. But boys being boys, there were some exceptions to the rule. I remember the time when one of my innocent experiments went terribly wrong. I was playing on the roof, where we kept a couple of pet doves, when I decided to find out how fast an object would drop to the street after I released it from my towering vantage point. So, I chose a heavy hammer from my tool-box (I loved making things out of wood, and had a complete set of tools at my disposal) and threw it over the wall that ran around the perimeter of the roof. Fortunately, no one got hit with my missile. Unfortunately, the hammer bounced off the pavement and, for no good reason at all, decided to fly straight through one of the large and very expensive display-windows in the front of the store. That was the time that I receiving a good whipping from father.

The city of Znojmo is surrounded by a remarkable countryside. First there is the Dyie River that flows through one part of the town. Then there are lush forests, fertile fields, beautiful orchards, large vineyards and many recreational areas. We swam in the Dyje River (it was within walking distance from the store), and went on day trips into the nearby forests any time father was able to take off from his grueling schedule. We picked mushrooms and ran after butterflies whenever we emerged into meadows full of wild flowers. And when we stopped to rest, father liked to whittle twigs that he transformed, in no time at all, into whistles capable of producing clear, shrill sounds.

We also spent many happy times with our extended family in Kravsko, and enjoyed the company of our Viennese cousins, Susanne and Ruth, whenever their parents came down to visit. One summer season, Aunt Johanna rented an apartment in downtown Znojmo, and we actually became fond of having them constantly around, even though they were mere girls.

Visits with our family in Lostice were, as I mentioned

earlier, quite infrequent. I guess that was because it took several hours to get there and father could not take too much time off from his responsibilities. Even on Sundays, when retail was closed, father regularly set up spot-checks of stores to find out whether any of them were having inventory shortages. Father worked seven days a week.

It was at the tender age of six years, during the 1936 school year, that I entered the first grade, and my days stopped being all fun and games. Still, it was not long before I adapted to the new routine, and to the new direction that my life was taking.

However, some time later, cracks started to appear in our peaceful universe, cracks that, in general, appeared insignificant. Yes, Europe's crisis evolved slowly at first, but then its ominous rumblings took on the life of a runaway locomotive. There was no stopping the world from tumbling into an abyss.

Father saw the danger for what it was, and decided to save our lives by taking the family out of the country. Fortunately, the company had just started a program that gave its Jewish employees top priority for job-openings outside Czechoslovakia, and father jumped at the opportunity. And to move matters along, father requested an immediate transfer from the Retail Division to the Import/ Export Division named Kotva (Czech name for anchor) because it was in the process of a vigorous expansion, and was opening new branches all over the world.

His request was approved in due time and, once again, new challenges were set in motion for our family. Father was assigned to a lesser job, one that allowed him to report regularly to Zlin, for Kotva's orientation meetings on procedures and intricacies of the import/export business. He became the manager of a small store in Zidenice, a suburb of Brno.

We moved to Brno during the early part of 1938, an astounding city as far as I was concerned. The scope and cosmopolitan diversity surpassed anything else that I had experienced before. It was, and still is, the administrative and cultural capital of the Province of Moravia, and the second largest city in the country.

We had barely settled into our new home, when father was forced to leave for several weeks. It was not Zlin that required his presence that time. Being a reservist, he was recalled to temporary duty in the military. Czechoslovakia was determined to defend its borders against a potential german invasion.

I may be prejudiced, but father really was a dashing dragoon, and I have a picture to prove it. The photograph shows him in a standing position; he has a cap with a short visor on his head, a thin moustache on his upper lip and he is attired in a belted jacket, with a long sword clipped to the left side. He also holds a riding crop with his left hand, and a cigarette with the other. This is definitely a picture of the neatest cavalryman I had ever seen.

As I said before, Czechoslovakia mobilized because Hitler wanted to annex the Czech territory known as Sudeteland. It was ready to fight, even against the worst of odds, to prevent the break up of its territory and maintain its borders. It even formed alliances with France, England and other countries in the hope of safeguarding its independence. Unfortunately, nothing helped. In September of 1938, at the infamous meeting in Munich, the British Prime Minister Neville Chamberlain surrendered to Hitler's demands and sacrificed Czechoslovakia in the name of peace. Hitler had promised during the meeting that the Sudeteland would be his only territorial demands in Europe. But, as the World found out, this was just a ploy on his part. He grabbed the Sudeteland on September 19, 1938, and overran the rest of Czechoslovakia on March 14, 1939.

Fortunately for us, we managed to leave Czechoslovakia at the end of January, 1939, and narrowly escaped the Nazis by the skin of our teeth.

This is how it all came to pass.

After the reserve forces demobilized, and father returned home, he notified the office in Zlin that he wanted to get out of the country without further delays. He made it clear that he did not care where he would be transferred, as long as he could leave within weeks.

And so, as I mentioned at the beginning of this Memoir, the first position that became available was the one in Romania. Father "grabbed" it without hesitation, and arranged to have our travel documents processed on an emergency basis. At the same time, our parents started to grapple with another dilemma. They had to think about what to take along to our new destination, and what to leave behind. Eventually, practicality won over sentimentality, and they decided to leave most of our possessions in the good

care of relatives. We were going to take only what we could
fit in our personal luggage. After all, it was not as if we were
leaving for good. A couple of years, at most, and we should
be back home, reunited once more with those cherished
possessions.

However, things did not work out as planned. To
father's dismay, the family passports were lost during visa
processing at the Romanian Embassy and, by the time new
ones were issued, the Romanian position had been given
to some one else. Of course, this was really a blessing in
disguise because Romania eventually became as unsafe as
any other country in Europe.

The very next opening that materialized was the one in
the Congo, and that was how we landed in Elisabethville, the
major town in Congo's southeastern province of Katanga.
Father's assignment was to open the second Kotva branch in
the colony. The first one, in the capital city of Leopoldville,
was performing beyond all expectations, and the company
wanted to cash in on that success.

Our new travel documents were issued during the
month of December 1938, in a passport office right in
downtown Zlin, By the way, this clearly shows the clout
that Bata wielded with the Czech authorities. Think of it,
in order to accommodate the company, the government
maintained a passport office in Zlin, a private company town.

Father spent a couple of weeks in Zlin, for final briefings
and for some general information about the Congo.
However, once we reached our destination, it became
obvious that the personnel in the export department had

absolutely no clue about that particular area of the world. For instance, when father expressed his concerns about starting a brand new Kotva office in a strange country with a foreign language, he was told that there was nothing to worry about. To start with, the retail manager in Elizabethville had already been instructed to rent a good suite of offices for Kotva, and a suitable home for the family. Second, problems related to actual business could be worked out during frequent visits to Leopoldville. All father had to do was hop on the train once he closed the office on Friday evening, get all the advice he needed during an overnight stay in Leopoldville, and be home by opening time on Monday morning. Little did they know that there was no direct train connection between Elizabethville and Leopoldville, and that the round-trip journey would have taken father several weeks to accomplish. It is a rail and river route, where trains are used only to get around the non-navigable portions of the Congo River. Most of the trip is spent on paddle-wheel boats that sail cautiously over the ever-changing navigation channels during daylight hours, and drop anchor near riverbanks the minute it gets dark. This trek stretches for some 1500 miles.

By the way, in accordance with Congolese regulations, the company had to give father a three-year contract, so he could become eligible for work and residency permits in the colony. Another part of these rules required that, at the end of the three years, employees were given six-months of paid leave in a temperate-climate region (usually the employees' country of origin), before resuming work in the tropics.

This was deemed essential for the continued good health of employees and their dependents.

The immigration rules also required that we submit to thorough physical examinations, and be immunized against various tropical diseases. All of this took place over several days in the outpatient section of Zlin's large hospital, and so we stayed at the company's hotel for the duration of the procedures. It was not a lavish hotel, but it was thoroughly modern and exceptionally well run. It was regularly overrun with businessmen from all over the world.

In any event, we finally left on the first leg of our long journey at the end of January, 1939. We took the train from Prague to Antwerp, by way of Brussels. I remember Uncle Arnold standing on the quay and waving goodbye as we pulled out of Prague's railroad terminal. Little did I realize at the time that it would be another thirteen years before I would see him again, this time in the USA, at the opposite side of the Atlantic Ocean. It was when Harry and I flew from the Congo to the States, early in 1952, to visit our relatives and to see for ourselves what that famous country was all about.

It was during that trip that I became totally captivated with the States, and decided right then and there that I would return, for good, the minute I could make it happen.

Anyway, after the train emerged from Prague's cavernous depot and we eventually tired of gaping out of the window, we stowed our luggage in the overhead rack and made ourselves comfortable for the long journey. Harry and I played a board game while our parents remained unusually quiet, or so I thought, as the train rolled toward our first stop, the German border. They were evidently sad at leaving, but they must have been relieved that we were finally getting out of harm's way.

Some time later, the train stopped across the border, right inside German territory, the country ruled by Hitler and his Nazi hordes. And yet, I do not remember experiencing any particular bouts of foreboding at the time, not even after what I saw next. The compartment door opened abruptly and a huge man, he must have been well over six feet tall, stepped boldly inside and instantly gave that hideous Nazi hand salute. He was dressed in an impeccable uniform, complete with the ugly swastika armband on his left sleeve and a side arm at his belt. Nonetheless, he was quite civil and actually processed our travel documents with professional courtesy. When he was done, he gave another Nazi hand salute, and firmly closed the compartment door on his way out. But, while the border crossing was uneventful for our family, others were not as fortunate. We heard that a number of passengers were not allowed to transit through Germany, and were forced to return to Czechoslovakia.

After changing trains in Brussels, we reached Antwerp on schedule, only to be told that our sailing date had been pushed back by a whole week because of some engine troubles on the vessel. This was unfortunate, not because we were reluctant to spend extra time in Antwerp, the center of Flemish culture for hundreds of years, but because father did not have much cash to pay for the unexpected layover (fiscal

regulations had allowed only limited funds to be taken out
of Czechoslovakia). Nonetheless, we managed to enjoy our
extended time in Antwerp, even though we had to spend the
week in a small and unassuming hotel, and had our meals at
inexpensive restaurants. We saw the Cathedral of Our Lady,
with its three monumental altarpieces painted by Peter Paul
Rubens, the Grand Square (Grote Market) dominated by
the Golden Age Town Hall and the Jewish neighborhood
of Joodse-wijk that was teeming with black-coated ultra
orthodox jewish men.

Language was not much of a problem because
many Flemish people understood enough German to
communicate with our parents. By the way, three languages
are spoken in Belgium; namely French (Walloon), Flemish
and, to a much lesser degree, German. The latter is the
regional language of a miniscule part of Belgium and does
not wield the same influence as the other two languages.
Both the Flemish and the French ethnic groups are
extremely touchy about their heritage, and neither will
tolerate discrimination in any form whatsoever. For instance,
when the post office brings out new stamps, it has to make
sure that half of each issue is printed with, for instance,
"Belgique" on top of the design and "Belgie" underneath,
while the other half of the issue has the names reversed the
other way around. Both, French and Flemish are the two
official languages of Belgium.

At last, our sailing date came, and we took a cab to the
harbor and our liner, the SS Leopoldville. That turned out
to be one of the most exciting days of my young life.

The date was February 13, 1939.

It was going to take me many years before I would walk once more on the European Continent.

7. Escape to Africa

The Compagnie Maritime Belge, the main link between Belgium and the Colony, owned a number of medium-size vessels, all named after Congolese cities, and collectively known as the "Congo Boats". It used these ships to provide reliable mail deliveries to the Congo, and maintain a regular passenger service with the colony. By the way, it was only on February 27, 1946, that airmail and regular passenger service were finally set up between Leopoldville and Brussels, on Sabena's DC-4 airplanes (Sabena was the Belgian National Airline that also flew passengers in the interior of the Congo). The flights took twenty-five hours, twenty-five very long and uncomfortable hours. I know that well, as I was on one of those never-ending flights, and can vividly remember the suffocating desert heat that hit me when I stepped off the plane in Kano, Nigeria. The plane was refueled and cleaned during the Kano stop, while the passengers were given breakfast with some very strong coffee. I could not wait to leave that overheated place. Additional information about this flight will be given in another chapter.

The itinerary for the ocean trip to the Congo called for several ports-of-call. The first one was Lobito in the Portuguese colony of Angola, and then followed by the ports of Banana, Boma and Matadi in the Belgian Congo. Lobito was the jumping-off point for passengers going to Eastern Congo, while Matadi was used for the Western Congo. The trip from Antwerp to Lobito took two weeks. Lobito is where we were scheduled to leave th ship.

The SS Leopoldville, weighing 11,172 gross ton and stretching 501 feet in length, was all decked-out in multicolored pennants when I first caught a glimpse of her towering mass. She was moored at the traditional berth for the Congo Boats, along the side of one of the Scheldt River quays, in Antwerp's busy harbor. It was the largest "boat" that I had ever seen (I guess I expected something about the size of the boats plying the rivers and canals of Czechoslovakia). But, as I found later on, this was not merely a big and handsome vessel, it was a valiant one as well. It fought fearlessly throughout the war, up to its ultimate end, when it was sunk in proximity of the French port of Cherbourg. That happened during its 25th crossing of the English Channel, on Christmas Eve 1944, when a German torpedo hit it broadside. Some 700 men, out of the 2000 American troops on board, were lost in this tragic attack.

The embarkation process was lengthy and tiresome. Officials and porters were busy all over the quay, and passengers spent their last moments on land, to huddle together with family and friends that had come to see them off. There was a lot of excitement and exhilaration all over the place, but also sadness and even dread.

I could not help wondering how such mixed feelings could affect almost everyone on the quay. Obviously youth shields from reality.

When the ship's horn emitted a warning blast, all the stragglers rushed up the gangplank and stepped on board. But none went below decks. We all lined the handrails as the ship moved gently away from the dock, turned into Scheldt's main shipping channel and started its run toward the ocean.

The River Scheldt (the Escaut in French), which connects Antwerp to the North Sea, some 50 miles downstream, is extremely wide and carries a large volume of maritime traffic. This is the river that made Antwerp the second largest harbor in Europe, and one of the finest ports in the world.

As usual, the channel was very busy and vessels of all types and sizes were on the go all around us. We remained topside for the longest time, and went to our cabin only after we were no longer able to stand on our feet.

Our second-class cabin was of medium size, with two double beds, each with a privacy curtain (in case strangers shared the cabin). The steel ceiling held a fan and the bulkhead had a porthole that let us see the ocean. There were two washbasins, one on each side of the cabin, but shower and toilet facilities were located outside, at the end of the passageway.

The "Salle de Gymnastique" was rather compact, but it did have a couple of stationary bicycles, a rowing machine, weight lifting equipment and a punching ball.

The "Fumoir" (Smoking Lounge) was attractively appointed with lovely stained-glass panels on the walls and ceiling. A portion of the ceiling was built on hinges so it could be cranked open to clear the smoke and allow fresh air into the lounge. It was ingenious and quite effective. The furniture was very comfortable and I watched many exciting card games that went on at all hours of the day and night.

The "Pouponniere" (Nursery-Playroom) had little chairs and tables grouped around a hopscotch game that was painted right on the steel floor. The room contained two large bins full of toys for small kids.

The decks were lined with comfortable folding chairs and some of the areas were set aside for various activities. There was the sports deck, the promenade deck, etc.

Life on board had a good beginning. First and foremost, it meant that I was finally on an ocean liner that was sailing toward that distant and mysterious Africa, the Africa of my dreams. Then, there was that marvelous experience with our first trip to the dining room. The meal consisted of the most tempting and succulent dishes (I have never seen such variety of pastry and ice cream in my whole life), and it became immediately obvious that fine dining was going to be the major activity of our trip. We really enjoyed those first hours on board.

But our feelings of contentment and wellbeing did not last long, and our comfort level started to deteriorate quickly once we reached the huge Western Scheldt Estuary and moved into the rough North Sea. The ship begun to pitch in an imperceptible way at first, but as we sailed on, this became more noticeable and our discomfort became more intrusive. And it did not take long before I started to feel woozy. Unfortunately, things got worst before they got better. As luck would have it, we sailed right into a tenacious storm that dogged us for three full days. The high seas tossed us about like a cork, and made the ship roll from side to side with tiresome monotony. We promptly succumbed to seasickness, the worst misery known to man as far as I am concerned. I almost wished to die right then and there, to get rid of that terrible agony. Fortunately (as if anything could be fortunate under these foul circumstances), the constant roll of the ship kept us in a state of absolute exhaustion, an exhaustion that helped us doze through some of the worst stages of the storm.

Once the storm abated and the seas calmed down, most of us quickly regained our sea legs, and once again started to enjoy life onboard. I said "most of us" because father was unfortunately unable to shake off the lingering effects of his seasickness, and remained uncomfortable all the way to Lobito.

As far as Harry and I were concerned, the on-board activities were ready made for the two of us. We played shuffle board, table tennis, cards and all kinds of board games. Personally, I also liked to lie on a deck chair and peek through the handrail at the rushing ocean. What amazed me was that the "footprint" of the ship's wake remained in the water long after we moved on. How could an imprint last on such a fluid surface?

Two interesting events altered the daily routine of our trip. The first one was the Abandon Ship drill that was held early on, and the other was the Rite of Passage Through the Equator, which was celebrated half way through our journey. The Rite of Passage is an ancient naval custom, one that is observed, to this day, by most sailors.

The Abandon Ship drill was thorough and well planned. Each passenger was assigned to a particular lifeboat and trained on the proper use of a lifejacket. We were told firmly that, once the alarm was heard over the public address system, we were to drop whatever we were doing and assemble promptly at our specific lifeboat location.

The second interesting event, the right of passage, was one that added real excitement to our routine.

As we progressed in our voyage, the days became longer and the temperature started to rise noticeably. We were nearing the equator which divides the earth in two equal parts, between the North and the South Poles, i.e. the Northern and Southern Hemispheres. And when we were about to cross that imaginary line, the ship's company became busy planning for the ceremony honoring King Neptune, and for the compulsory initiation rites that were to be administered to those crossing the equator for the very first time (they were known as "Polliwogs"). Once a sailor goes through the required ritual, he becomes a "Shellback".

Mythology makes us believe that King Neptune, the Roman god of the ocean (Greeks called him Poseidon), rules over all the waters of the earth. Sailors crossing the equator for the first time must appear before him, and show why they should become future subjects of the ocean. Once initiated, they emerge as the adopted sons of King Neptune, and receive full authority to haze all Polliwogs on future crossings of the equator.

King Neptune is usually dressed in flowing garments,

with a crown on his head and a long beard across his face. He carries a three-pronged spear called the "trident", and holds court with his son Triton by his side. The King's retinue stands respectfully around the throne, and helps the King hand out the various trials and punishments that a Polliwog must go through in order to become a Shellback.

There are two levels of hazing, one for the ship's company and one for the passengers. The passengers are subjected to an easygoing type of hazing that promotes good humor, and consists of harmless ordeals that, at worst, are only moderately embarrassing and only slightly physical in nature. For instance, there are absurd characters to impersonate, funny tunes to vocalize, quinine to taste (there is nothing more acrid in the world), etc.

But, by contrast, sailors are treated harshly and without the least compassion during the entire hazing process. The ordeals reserved for them are unpleasant, occasionally offensive and definitely grueling. There is lathering with grease and tar, crawling through slop, cutting or dyeing of hair, and other preposterous trials meant to leave a lasting impression on the unfortunate candidates.

One more thing needs to be said about the equator. While it is the mid-line on the globe, it is also the latitude where the earth's seasons reverse; when it is winter in the north of the quator, it is summer in the south. For us, that meant that we had transitioned, within a few days, from Europe's chilly winter right into Africa's hot and humid summer. Initially, the change was not perceptible, but eventually the intense heat and burning sun became hard to tolerate. Our cabin, without air-conditioning (remember that this was in 1939), became really uncomfortable and we ended up spending all our waking hours topside, under the canopy that covered the deck.

And suddenly, here was our last day on board. It was marked by the crew's scramble to prepare the ship for next day's early arrival in port, and by the Lobito passengers packing their possessions.

As for me, I could hardly believe that the magic day, the day I so longed for, was finally within reach, and that I was going to take my first steps on the African mainland within the next few hours. The anticipation was killing me, and sleep eluded me for a while during that final night in our stuffy cabin.

Then morning came and, as I awakened, I could tell that something had changed. The ship was not moving. We had arrived. Still half asleep, I clambered topside and found that we were actually moored to a pier in the Angolan port of Lobito.

After two weeks on the ocean, here was Africa at last.

8. First Glimpse of Afirica

Harry had also come topside and, standing side by side, we gaped at the incredible hustle and bustle all along the dock. The unfamiliar sounds and sights were so unique that it took some time before our senses were capable of taking them all in. But that was not the case with the sickening stench that hit both of us fast and hard. And though we did not know it at the time, it appears that we had just been exposed to a strong "essence" of drying fish (drying acts as a preservative and keeps the fish edible for several weeks) mixed, for good measure, with decaying sea-creatures and rotting vegetation. This was a combination of overpowering smells, and it assaulted our nostrils with the foulest odor we had ever encountered.

Still, my dismay over the pervasive foul odor dissipated quickly enough, and I was able to re-focus my attention on the colorful tableau that stretched all over the dock at our feet. And I immediately became conscious of the fact that I was gawking right there at more black people than I had ever seen before in my whole life. Most of the men wore ordinary shorts with an occasional shirt or undershirt. But the women's outfits were anything but ordinary. They wore vividly colored wrap-around pieces of cloth (called "pagnes" in French), and whenever they moved out of a shaded area

into a fiery shaft of bright sunlight, they seemed to burst
into a flood of multi-colored lights (a boyish mind is full of
imagination). Amazingly, it appeared that each pagne was
dyed in its own combination of bright colors, because none
of them looked alike to me.

The next thing I noticed was that both the men and
the women carried almost everything on their heads. And
while some used their hands to keep the various items from
falling off, others kept their loads safe by merely holding
their heads level and their backs ramrod straight (isn't that
what fashion models practice in order to develop a perfect
posture?). Several of the women carried babies on their
backs, held comfortably in place by pieces of cloth wrapped
tightly around their bodies.

Various groups of white people were making their way
to the ship, and I instantly noticed the sun helmets on their
heads. That was when I remembered, with somewhat of a
thrill, that we had bought our own helmets in Antwerp, and
that I shall be wearing one myself when we disembarked
later that day. The expats that were coming on board must
have completed their tour of duty in the tropics, and were
taking the ship back to Europe for a well-deserved leave.

Tropical sun helmets are made from a strong cork
compound. They are lightweight and, for added protection,
have brims that guard the wearer's face and the nape of his
neck from the unforgiving sun. They must be worn from
eight in the morning until four in the afternoon because that
is when the danger of strokes is at the highest. I am talking
about sunstrokes that are caused by an excessive exposure to

the sun, and are usually the source of grim health problems. The stricken person becomes temporarily unconscious and usually ends up being paralyzed. I witnessed this when, many years later, it struck down a family friend playing in a soccer match in Leopoldville. He was one of a number of reckless Europeans who did not care about wearing sun helmets and was running around the field without proper head protection. He lost consciousness and was immediately rushed to the hospital, where he remained until flown back to Europe. Unfortunately, he had to endure complete paralysis for the rest of his life.

Before concluding my remarks about sunstrokes, I should mention the insidious aspect of the danger. Insidious because sunstrokes strike in a random way and give no warnings. For instance, a person may decide, from time to time, to venture out into the sun without a helmet. Experiencing no problems, he becomes nonchalant about the whole thing and decides against using a sun helmet altogether. But one day, without any indication, the sun's rays might strike his head at the wrong angle, ruining his health and devastating the rest of his life.

Anyway, as we were about to rejoin our parents, Harry gave a yell and pointed to something on the dock, near the gangplank. I gave a look in the direction of his finger and burst out laughing so hard that my sides started to ache. A native had just left the gangplank with a large legal envelope held fast on his head by the weight of a large umbrella. As I found out later, this was the quintessential African messenger.

Eventually, we tore ourselves away from the railing and rejoined our parents in the cabin. They had just finished packing the remainder of our personal items and were ready to go to breakfast. That was to be our last meal on board.

After breakfast there were all kinds of time-consuming formalities that father took care of; such as settling up with the ship's purser, completing Angola's Transit and Customs formalities, etc.

It was shortly before noon that we left the ship.

9. Lobito

We stepped off the covered gangplank into the sweltering sun, and proceeded to a hotel that was within a short walking distance from the ship. All the passengers bound for Eastern Congo were assembling there for lunch and the ensuing boarding of the train that was to take them to their final destination in the very heart of Africa.

However, before talking about our train journey, I shall mention a couple of interesting facts about Angola, and say something about the rest of our day in Lobito.

Angola's coastal region, except for the brief period from 1641 to 1648, has been under Portuguese rule from 1575 to1975. During the few years in question, the Dutch tried to set up their own coastal stations in that region because they needed to provide support for their oceangoing trade between Europe and Asia. Their efforts failed and they left the coast. The Portuguese colony was eventually named Angola, and the city of Luanda (Sao Paulo de Loanda) became its capital. Luanda is still a capital, but in 1975 it became the capital of the Republic of Angola. Luanda is a major port with a bustling metropolitan center and beautiful sandy beaches that extend up and down the coast. Tragically though, it is a city with a dreadful past. For some 200 years, it had been the hub of the slave trade between Portuguese

Africa and Brazil.

I can personally attest to the charm of Luanda's sandy beaches because I enjoyed them for several days over the 1953/1954 New Year's holiday. I had earned my pilot's license in the Congo just a few months earlier, and had decided to undertake a long-distance flight over the holidays. I picked Luanda because I had heard that it was an attractive city, and because I wanted to spend time at the ocean (the ocean is quite a draw for anyone living in the interior of Africa). However, once I had made my decision, I became a little apprehensive about what I was getting into. As an inexperienced pilot, I was going to fly for the first time through an international border, and I was going to spend several hours flying V.F.R. (Visual Flight Rules) over a large swath of unknown territory. Visual Flight Rules are the flight guidelines used by pilots that have only a rudimentary compass on board (magnetic compass), and nothing else to guide them to their destination. I had no electronic equipment in my Piper Super Cruiser, not even a basic radio to request landing instructions upon my descent into Luanda's airport (in a future chapter I will talk about flying in the Congo "by-the-seat-of-my-pants"). But, I rose to the challenge and successfully plotted my course with good landmarks for points-of-reference. Also, I arranged for the refueling of the plane and for customs clearance formalities at Matadi's airport, the only projected stop in the Congo. It took two hours to fly from Leopoldville to Matadi, with another three hours to get to Luanda. The Super Cruiser came from the Aero Club Royal du Congo Belge, and since

I was one of the member pilots, I was able to sign it out for a whole week at a very low cost. By the way, Harry and a mutual friend went along on this flight.

We reached Luanda in one piece and, after clearing customs, took a cab to our hotel. We spent the rest of that day on the beach, ate an early dinner, and literally collapsed in our beds. It had been a long day.

Our vacation started well, but it became even better after I flew the manager of our hotel, and his photographer, over the city so they could take aerial photos and have new post cards printed for the hotel's gift shop. From then on we were given full use of the hotel's limousine, enjoyed freely all of the hotel's amenities, and even became the guests of honor at the unforgettable New Year festivities that lasted well into the wee hours of the morning. Those were the times great memories are made of. Anyway, I wonder whether the hotel, the Grand Hotel Universo, is still in business and whether the gift-shop still offers the aerial postcards that were made so many years ago.

Now, let us return to Lobito and our short stroll from the ship to the hotel. Although brief, this first walk among Africans was absolutely thrilling for me. Of course, I was immediately struck by the fact that most of them wore no shoes on their feet and that they appeared totally unaffected by the heated pavement of the dock. Then I saw an Albino. He was a young man with milky-white skin, white hair and pinkish eyes that he kept half closed against the sun's bright light. I understand that this condition is due to a deficiency of pigment or dark coloring matter, and that it is inherited. I also saw many light-colored natives. They were mulattos, the children of mixed marriages. I really did not know where to look first and had a difficult time keeping up with the rest of the family.

As we reached the hotel, a single story whitewashed building topped with an oversized roof, and made ourselves comfortable on its huge veranda, I finally got an unobstructed view of the harbor that had welcomed us to Africa. It was a sweeping natural harbor protected by a breakwater sandbar over 3 miles long, with a 700 yard-wide navigable channel at its entrance. This wide channel allowed vessels to proceed to the port's deep-water berths without pilots or tugboats.

A strong ocean breeze kept us fairly comfortable during the sumptuous lunch that was served on the vast veranda. The tables were covered with crisp white tablecloths and the napkin holders were large ivory rings with beautiful carvings. But it was the African waiters that most impressed us. They were efficient and responsive to all our needs, even though we had to communicate with them by gestures, as they understood only the Portuguese language. They were dressed in white shirts and shorts. But, as you may have guessed by now, they were all barefoot.

Our first meal on African soil was unforgettable and, if this was a harbinger of things to come, we had little to fear about our future lives in the tropics (strictly my own opinion at the time).

When the departure time drew closer, we finished our refreshments and moved leisurely to the adjacent rail-siding

where the Benguela train was being readied for the long
journey into the interior of the continent. The trip was
to take three full days, and would cover some 1,400 miles
from Lobito to Elisabethville. By the way, due to a unique
agreement between the Compagnie Maritime Belge and
the Benguela Railway, that particular train was reserved
exclusively for the passengers who arrived from Antwerp,
and no one else was allowed to board it either in Lobito or
during the entire trip. The train stopped only to replenish its
wood and water supplies, both of which the gigantic steam
locomotive used in considerable amounts.

By the way, "Benguela" is also the name of the ocean
current that draws icy waters from the South Ocean and
carries them northward along the South West Coast
of Africa. Because they release only small amounts of
evaporation, these icy waters do not generate the heavy rain
clouds that warmer ocean waters produce in other regions of
the coast. Accordingly, the Benguela Current is responsible
for the parching of South West Africa and is the primary
cause for the Kalahari and Namib Deserts.

Once we climbed on board the train, we were shown
to a nice Pullman compartment, with a washbasin and a
small folding table. It was clean and appeared comfortable
enough for a three-day journey. However, when we returned
from the dining car later that evening, it had become quite
cramped. The porter had turned the compartment into a
sleeper for four, by locking the two top berths into their
horizontal positions. During the day these berths were kept
out of the way, flush against the side bulkheads, adding much

room to the compartment.

One real drawback was the lack of a bathroom within the privacy of our compartment. We had to use the public shower and toilet in the passageway, at the end of the rail car. If it had not been for that, I would have felt right at home during that long trip.

Construction on the Benguela Railway started in 1903, but reached the Congo area only in 1928. The snail-like progress was caused by the ruggedness of the route. From Lobito, the line runs across a narrow coastal plain for some 30 to 40 miles, before it climbs abruptly up a steep escarpment to a large inland plateau, part of which tops out at 8,596 feet. That escarpment is so sheer that a five-mile stretch of the track had to be made into a rack-and-pinion section. Many years later that section was converted to a normal track, however, even with today's powerful locomotives, lower loads must be used on that sheer grade.

The Benguela Railway had to resolve other difficulties.

One such difficulty was the problem of maintaining a steady supply of water for the trains. Sufficient supply was rather unreliable on the semi-arid plateau, and the railway had to drill deep wells to find adequate water for the passengers and thirsty locomotives.

Then there was the need for large stock-piles of firewood. That need was resolved by large plantations of fast growing eucalyptus trees that the railroad set up at various points along the route.

The first day in Africa tired me out completely. That night, I fell asleep before my head hit the pillow in one of the top berths of our compartment. The monotonous clicking of the wheels kept me in a very deep sleep, so much so that I did not witness the train's laborious climb up the escarpment, and missed its final thrust upon the edge of the plateau. When I woke up, the train was winding its way through a panorama of grasslands, and the sun's bright rays were bouncing brightly across our compartment.

After a solid breakfast, we settled on a daily routine that kept us pleasantly occupied over the whole journey. The meals in the dining car were totally enjoyable; the food and the service were excellent. For instance, I remember that we had, in addition to all kinds of African fruits (I love fruits), fresh strawberries that grow at certain elevations in the tropics. The waiters were well trained and quick to grin. In their impeccable white jackets and gloves, they kept pouring refreshments no matter how much time we spent at our table.

Whenever the train stopped to re-supply the locomotive with water and wood, natives swarmed up and down the tracks with woven baskets full of local fruits and small handicrafts that they tried to peddle before we resumed our trip. They hawked their wares to any passenger who leaned outside the window of his compartment. Moreover, a throng of persistent vendors would assail anyone who decided to step outside the Pullman. As might be expected, prices dropped the minute the whistle announced the imminent departure of the train.

Our time in the compartment was spent reading, and playing games. But we also did a lot of gazing at the exotic

African countryside that was passing by our window. All those majestic palm trees and small villages of mud huts and thatched roofs were fascinating. But I promptly became disappointed because, no matter how many hours I spent at the window, I failed to see a single monkey, a single lion, or even a single antelope... not one of the animals of my dreams. In the end, I consoled myself by concluding that the deafening noise of our passage drove the animals away from the vicinity of the tracks, and that I would end up seeing a lot of them once we reached the Congo. Hope runs eternal in a young mind.

Time flew by, and all of a sudden we rolled into Dilolo, the Congolese border-crossing post where passengers had to go through customs and immigration.

We had not, as yet, reached the ultimate destination of Elisabethville. However, we were finally in the Belgian Congo, the country where we thought we would live for about three years. But it turned out that this was, in fact, the country where I would grow up and reach manhood. And though it was untamed and largely uncivilized, I became very fond of it. It was the country that we escaped to, it was the country that saved us from the Nazi hell that eventually engulfed most of Europe, and other parts of the World.

10. Africa and the Congo

Now that we have reached the Congo, I think it fitting to give some information about Africa in general, and the Belgian Congo in particular.

The continent of Africa is second in size only to Asia. And yet, no more than 200 years ago it was still referred to as the Dark Continent because the interior remained a land of total mystery ("dark" is the code for "absolutely no clue of what it is"), even though the coasts had already been explored to some degree. Nothing much was known about the heart of the continent, its peoples or animals, despite the fact that portions of the African and European coasts lie only nine miles apart, right across the Strait of Gibraltar. And even when we got there in 1939, large tracts of the deep interior were pretty wild, essentially unexplored, and entirely unaffected by civilization. It was the Romans that coined a name for the continent, after they conquered what is known today as Tunisia. They used the Berber tribe's name "Afri", and came out with Africa.

There were many hurdles that held up the exploration of the African interior. The huge land was practically impenetrable. Vast deserts, jungles and the scarcity of navigable rivers posed enormous difficulties to the white man. The Sahara Desert in the North, and the Namib

Desert in the South, were expressly formidable obstacles to overcome, and expeditions moving up the Nile River were defeated by the great cataracts at Aswan. On the West Coast, insurmountable rapids, no more than100 miles from the mouth of the Congo River, dead ended that route to the interior. And yet I believe that the paramount difficulty in all this was that the continent was rife with rare diseases fatal to explorers. In my opinion, it was the latter that prevented the Europeans from ruling the African continent prior to the eighteenth century. Actually, people went so far as to say that the Rain Forest nurtured frightful diseases as a defense against the white man's invasion of its domain.

The list of diseases encountered on the African continent is long and, unfortunately, ever widening. For instance, Ebola and AIDS, some of the most lethal diseases afflicting humanity today, surfaced on that continent only in the recent past. Yet, people at large still associate Africa primarily with the following dreaded tropical diseases;

Leprosy- This is one of the oldest diseases known to man. It assails the body's nerves, skin and mucous membranes, and is often very painful. In advanced stages it weakens the body until it falls prey to other diseases, especially gangrene. Gangrene attacks the fingers and other body extremities, and produces the terrible disfiguration that is the haunting characteristic of leprosy.

Malaria- Worldwide, more deaths are caused by malaria than any other disease. Some estimates claim that one million lives are lost each year, with some

90 percent of them in Africa. It is the females of the "anophele" mosquitoes that bite people and pass malaria parasites from an infected person to a healthy one. These mosquitoes have a perfectly good reason for doing this (good reason as far as the females are concerned), since they require the protein from human blood to lay their eggs. Male mosquitoes live off such things as the sap of trees, and they do not bother human beings. Customarily, these mosquitoes thrive in sweltering environments, and that was why early European colonizers believed that the disease was transmitted by the putrid air found in the swamps and rain forests of the tropics (the word malaria was coined from the words "mal air", which means hazardous/foul air).

Sleeping Sickness- A dreaded disease that is transmitted by the tsetse fly (long-bodied pest with a painful bite, and the size of a deer fly), and which is extremely dangerous to man and beast. It kills cattle, horses, and all manner of game, and impedes any attempts at improving the natives' economic and living conditions in the infected areas. In its final stages it invades the brain, inducing sleep and coma. Hence, that is where the name of Sleeping Sickness came by.

Yellow Fever- This infectious disease, transmitted from person to person by a particular type of mosquitoes, attacks the liver and digestive tract. One of the usual symptoms of the disease is jaundice, and obviously that became the rationale for naming it the

"Yellow Fever".

Elephantiasis- Here again, a particular species of mosquitoes transmits this disease. The parasite enters the body's lymphatic vessels and causes grotesquely swollen limbs, debilitating fevers and excruciating pain.

As a footnote to this list of diseases, I can not help but wonder what a better world this would be if all the species of mosquitoes could be eliminated from the surface of the earth. Horrible diseases would disappear and untold lives would be saved. So then, why is it that the world does not declare an all out war against them? After all, it has been shown during the 1950's that malarial infection rates quickly fell wherever DDT, or other potent insecticides, were used in targeted areas. Humanity should throw all its resources at the problem, without wasting money and efforts on stop gap measures.

Before leaving the issue of diseases, I should mention something called the "African Sickness". It is so called because the white man's privileged life in the tropics, with its unhurried and easy-going pace, traps the individual forever in the web of colonial niceties, and has him longing for Africa whenever he leaves the continent. It takes away a person's ability to tolerate the structured life in Europe and, more often than not, compels him to live out his retirement years in the colony.

And this brings me to declare unequivocally that Africa is not merely a snake-infested and sultry wilderness full of terrible diseases and untold dangers. It is, as well, an exotic and dazzling continent brimming with the world's most remarkable variety of landscapes and animal life. It has stunning vistas, high mountains with impressive snow-capped peaks, lakes that are some of the largest and deepest in the world, immense forests, vast savannahs teaming with wild life, harsh deserts and majestic rivers. It is home to a variety of people, from the giant Masai with their impressive height of almost seven-feet, to the Pygmies that reach only a little over four-feet tall. It supports the largest land animals of the world, and some of those, such as the mighty gorilla, the tall giraffe and the huge hippopotamus, can not be found anywhere else on earth.

There are several species of animals that live only in the Congo. For instance, there is the lowland gorilla and the Bonobo. The Bonobo is said to be the ape that is the most closely related to humans. Another example is the okapi. This is a forest dwelling animal related to the giraffe, about the size of a zebra, with a giraffe-shaped head and white zebra-like stripes on its hindquarters. It lives a solitary life in the Itury Forest, along the Congo River, and is the country's national symbol.

Now something needs to be said about the crawling creatures that inspire such horror in most people - the snakes of Africa. There are over one hundred species of them, but some of the most frightful serpents are the cobras and the vipers, since their poisons are extremely potent. The cobra's venom is neurotoxic, it acts on the nervous system and death occurs rapidly, generally due to heart failure. The viper's poison destroys blood cells and body tissues, causing extensive internal bleeding. And while they are grouped together with some 12 extremely poisonous "hooded' snakes, they are remarkably dissimilar in many ways:

The cobra is thin, active, rather nervous, and it lays eggs. The spitting cobra, one of the most peculiar snakes in the world, is a member of this family of reptiles. It instinctively aims at the face, and very accurately delivers the poison from a distance of several feet. When the poison touches the eyes, it triggers excruciating pain and, if not treated in time, will cause permanent blindness. But this cobra can also injects its venom in the usual way, by burying its teeth into the flesh of a prey. Its fangs are short and erect.

The viper is quite different from the cobra. It is fat, lazy and rather placid. The viper's fangs are very long and hinged in order to lie along the roof of its mouth when not in use. It gives birth to live baby vipers, it does not lay eggs.

These brief comments on Africa would be incomplete without some notes about the palm tree and the dugout canoe. Both of these play important roles in the lives of the natives and in the economy of the continent.

There are many types of palm trees, such as the oil, date, and coconut. But among all of them, the most valuable and, as it turns out, the most common in tropical lands, is the oil palm tree. It produces its fruit when it reaches five years of age, and continues doing so for almost one hundred years. This fruit is about the size of a date, and has a tough stringy outer layer that surrounds a deep-red fleshy part. In the center of this fleshy part is a round pit that is rock-hard. The fruits grow in large clumps under the crown of the palms, right where the fronds fan out from the trunk.

When immature, they are fleshy, sweet and delicious to eat. However, when they mature, they become extremely hard and difficult to chew. But when the fleshy part is boiled, it releases the palm oil that is used in food and the production of soap and candles. Palm oil has a very pleasant odor, an amber-red color and is deemed supreme among edible oils. The pit, which is crushed under heavy pressure, produces a white-looking fat that is widely used in the making of margarine. But as if its fruit was not enough of a boon to man, the palm tree itself supplies many other necessities of life. It provides the timber and thatch to build huts, and the fibers that go into ropes and brooms. Narrow strips cut from its leaves are woven into hats, baskets and mats. And, of course, the tree also provides shade and fuel.

But ask any male of the population, and he will passionately declare that the palm tree's finest product is the palm wine that is extracted from the male tree. It is harvested like latex or maple syrup. The tapper climbs to the crown and cuts small channels in the trunk around the area where the male flower emerges from the tree. Using palm leaves as funnels, he directs the slow-dripping sap into gourds that were previously hung from appropriate palm fronds. These gourds are emptied twice a day, over a period of some three weeks, or for as long as the juice keeps flowing. The juice is thin and foamy when fresh, with a sweet but pungent taste. It is not very alcoholic at first, but after a day it begins to ferment and becomes quite intoxicating. But it must be said that, though the wine is very popular all over the tropics, it actually fits in the "acquired taste" classification of alcoholic drinks.

On second thought, I will also mention the Baobab tree before moving on to the dugout canoes.

The Baobab grows almost exclusively in Africa. It lives to a very old age, with some that are reputedly over two thousand years old. The thickness of its trunk is remarkable because it can reach a circumference of about thirty feet. It has large purple-and-white flowers, and its fruit, called "Bread Fruit" or "Monkey Bread", is almost a foot long. The fruit contains many seeds, surrounded by a mealy pulp that has a pleasant flavor and is good to eat. The tree's leaves and bark are used for medicines, and the bark's fibers are also used for cloth, rope and even a form of paper.

The dug-out canoe, or pirogue as it is called in the Congo, is still the quintessential mode of transportation in the African hinterland; roads are often impassable, and really few and far between. In the rainy season, cars get mired in deep mud. In the dry season, it is the sand that makes driving arduous and slow going. In any event, there is good evidence that dug-out canoes were used in Africa over 6,000 years ago, and there is no doubt that they are as important today as they were in that distant past. They range from a meager few feet in length, to a grand size of eighty feet, or more. I have personally observed large pirogues being moved swiftly along a river by over one hundred muscular oarsmen, all moving in perfect unison, all throwing their weight into every oar stroke. That scene never failed to impress me, no matter how often I saw it.

The men who fashion these canoes are real artisans.

They cut the tree to the desired length, square the two sides, and form the bow and the stern. A deep narrow groove is then hacked along the length of the log and wooden wedges are forced into the opening to keep the groove from closing. Finally, fire is set around the outside of the canoe and, as the heat dries the wood and expands the groove, large wedges are jammed deep into it in order to force the sides further apart and extend the girth of the canoe as much as possible.

And now, here is information about the Congo.

Congo, the heart of Africa, lies almost entirely within the Torrid Zone. The Equator stretches across the top third of the country and gives it the dubious reputation of being the sultriest tropical region on the continent. Within the narrow Equatorial belt, the rainy season reigns supreme for all twelve months of the year. The dry season begins to appear as distance increases from the Equator, and ultimately takes over the weather for up to six months, such as in the southern Province of Katanga, the area of the Colony that is the furthest from the Equator. The dry season is the "winter" season, with insignificant rainfall and cooler temperatures. Of course, major land features, such as the high plateau in the south-east, also influence the climate characteristics of the land.

Most of the country is a shallow basin drained by the mighty Congo River. Savannas cover large areas, especially in the south, with a variety of grasses and a scattering of small groups of trees. The Congo River is known as the Lualaba River when it emerges from Lake Mweru, in the south-eastern part of the country, and flows due north toward the equator, and the thunderous Stanley Falls located south of the town of Stanleyville. At Stanleyville, in the heart of the continent, it forms a great sweeping bend to the left, and takes on the name of the Congo River. It proceeds westward through some of the densest jungle on earth, before dipping south-west for its rendezvous with the great Atlantic Ocean. Stretching over 2,900 miles, it is one of the most majestic waterways of the world. And when it finally bursts into the Atlantic Ocean, it does so with such brute force that its mud-filled current is visible over a wide stretch of the ocean, and that it carves a 500 mile-long submarine canyon on the ocean floor that is 4,000 feet deep. However, even though it creates one of the largest natural harbors in Africa, it does not have a delta. It is relevant to remark at this point that practically all the important rivers on the African continent flow into the Atlantic. The two notable exceptions are the Nile that flows north into the Mediterranean, of course, and the Zambezi River that heads east into the Indian Ocean. The Zambezi is the river that creates the famous Victoria Falls, as it plunges some 400 feet off a cliff into a narrow gorge, on the border between Zambia and Zimbabwe.

The eastern edge of the Congo basin has a series of high hills and a string of large lakes that extend from south to north. The southern half of this area contains the richest mineral-bearing land in all Africa. The northern portion is known for the Itury Rain Forest that covers approximately a third of the region. It is one of the largest and thickest tropical rain forests in the world, and its canopy is so dense that sunlight rarely reaches some parts of the floor. The equator crosses the Itury, and creates the forest's hot and humid weather that persists throughout the year. The Congo River, which flows right through it, provides its chief mode of transport. The Itury is the home of the Mbuty tribe of Pygmies (the name comes from the Greek word Pygme, the measure of "half an arm's length). They are widely known as the "people of the arrow" because they use bows and arrows to hunt the animals that live in the towering canopy of the massive trees, and almost never venture close to the forest floor. The Pygmies' small build lets them move with stealth through the tangled undergrowth of bushes, vines and creepers, and allows them to hunt their prey without fear of detection. They are so good at concealment, that they actually hunt elephants with great success. They coat their bodies with elephant dung to deceive the animals' keen sense of smell, and lie in ambush behind trees until one of them comes within easy reach. They then creep behind the animal and, having cut its Achille's tendon, immobilize it helplessly in its track. At this point they pounce on the beast from all sides and, by mere strength of numbers, deliver the fatal blows (think about the irony of this, midgets of the human race taking on the giants of the forest). But this is a rare event and, in point of fact, the Pygmies live a harsh and difficult life because prey and edible vegetation, such as grains, fruits, roots and tubers, are scarce in the dark and inhospitable forest (wild honey is one of their favorite foods). They go naked, although occasionally they wear small leather loincloths, and live in igloo-shaped huts made of branches overlaid with large leaves that manage to keep the interior dry during the heaviest of down-pours. They are timid by nature and do not mix with non-pygmy tribes. Meat is swapped for manioc and other grains, but it is done without personal contact with outsiders. Pygmies place bush-meat, in the dead of night, outside the protective thorn-bush fence of a village, and return the following night to pick up the grains left there in exchange by the villagers.

In addition to its huge mineral wealth, which covers the gamut from diamonds and gold to copper, tin and radium, the Congo's natural resources include, among others, mahogany, rubber, palm oil, coffee, cocoa, cotton and sugar. The typical Africans live in villages of thatch-roofed mud huts, and are ruled by chieftains that have absolute control over their lives. The huts are built strictly for protection from the weather, with little consideration for comfort. All the cooking and most of the daily life take place outside the huts. The population supports itself with subsistence farming, hunting and fishing. The cassava plant, called manioc, is a major player in their diet. The plant's roots are rich in starch, but they also contain poisons that must be leached out before they can be processed into the flour that is used as the primary ingredient in most meals. Point of interest; women do much of the heavy work in the Congo, as in many other areas of Africa. Men, for their part, "exert" themselves at hunting and fishing. One of the species of fish that live in the Congo goes by the name of "Le Capitaine". They can weigh up to 150 pounds (I have seen many times where it took two grown men to carry one of these heavyweights) and are trapped occasionally, in large conical basket-like pods, by fishermen who live along rapids or falls. These woven pods, with their open ends facing upstream, are set in the midst of rushing waters that force the fish into the gaping holes and keep them trapped until the fishermen take them away. The fishermen use sturdy bamboo scaffoldings, which had been built over the rapids, to anchor the traps and to keep from being swept into the mighty current. It is quite an ingeneous setup.

Because of the sweltering heat and high humidity, the natives in the interior run about mainly naked (same as the pygmies in the Rain Forest), or use either loincloths or straw skirts. They adorn parts of their bodies with tattoos, clay paints and ornaments (Congolese coins, minted for the colony with perforated centers, become easily fashioned into creative ornaments). There is no shame or embarrassment in nudity, and no "logical" reason for clothing.

Some forms of body markings are used as tribal identification, and are achieved through tattooing, scarification, body piercing, distortion/stretching of ear lobes and lips, and filing of teeth.

Other body markings are the symbols of various initiations and rituals, namely circumcision, excision and others.

11. King Leopold II, David Livingstone, and Henry Morton Stanley

Three men, above all others, were directly involved in the creation of the Congo. One of them, King Leopold ll of the Belgians, personally took possession of the huge territory and forged his private fortune by exploiting the land without regard for fundamental justice or the welfare of the natives. Dr. David Livingstone and Henry Morton Stanley became involved through their exploration of the African Continent and, additionally on the part of Stanley, through his personal association with King Leopold II.

King Leopold ll (1835-1909) forged, in 1879, the Association Internationale du Congo which, despite its name, was actually Leopold's private organization, backed entirely by his own funds. The King utilized this organization to bolster his authority over the Congo basin, a region that Stanley had recently explored in his name. He subsequently claimed it as his own private realm, and the European Colonial Powers sanctioned this status-quo when they divvied up the African Continent at the Berlin conference of 1885. After all, the King had used his own money to finance Stanley's expeditions to the Congo River watershed, and his AIC had come up with a worthy humanitarian agenda for the area. As it was, the King lost no time in creating the "Congo Free State" (he even had a flag for his realm; a gold star in the midst of a blue field), and taking personal title to its immense natural and mineral wealth. He instituted a cruel colonial rule, and for some 20 years his agents treated the natives with outrageous atrocities and unrivaled brutality, essentially using a slave-labor approach to the plunder of the land. Eventually though, the world could no longer disregard such appalling acts against humanity, and protesters all over Europe started to agitate against the King's rule in Africa. Interestingly, what finally brought this injustice to the civilized world's awareness was George Washington Williams' cutting report titled "Open Letter to King Leopold" that he published in the 1890s. Williams, a black American Civil War veteran, had spent six months in the territory and used his first-hand knowledge to expose the cruelties perpetrated by the King's agents in the Congo. As a result, the King was ultimately forced to give up his private realm and to hand it over to Belgium. The Belgian Government took official possession of the territory on 11-15-1908 (quite grudgingly I may add, since the Belgians did not want to be drawn into an African adventure), and changed the name to the "Belgian Congo". Belgium instituted at once a paternalistic type of colonialism, suppressed inter-tribal warfare, fought slavery, set up a system of free medical services and engaged in building roads and railroads.

However, to his credit, I must mention that although King Leopold II was a greedy and autocratic king, he was also a man of vision. In 1898 he built, at his own expense, the outstanding Royal Museum for Central Africa in the small community of Tervuren, outside Brussels. He filled it with his large collection of African artifacts, field maps tediously hand-drawn by his agents, soil and rock samples from mineral rich areas, monkey skulls, stuffed fish and over six million bugs. Today's geologists use many of the maps and soil samples to assist global mining companies to pin-point Congo's vast riches of copper, cobalt, gold, tin and other mineral deposits. The museum contains a radioactive-proof bunker, protected by a steel door, which holds a 1,300-pound chunk of Congolese uranium from the same mine that produced the fuel for the nuclear bombs dropped on Japan at the end of World War II.

The second man in this trilogy of giants was Dr. David Livingstone (1813-1873), a Scottish medical missionary and a famous explorer of Africa. One of his goals was to find the source of the Nile. But, despite thirty years of wandering through jungles, swamps and savannas, he never attained that goal. He was able, however, to help clear up the mystery that surrounded the interior of the continent which, until then, was thought to be a vast desert. Of course, in reality it is anything but. Anyway, he went on his last expedition in 1865, and suddenly disappeared somewhere between Zanzibar (an island off the West Coast of Africa) and the region surrounding Lake Tanganyika. He was still trying, after many years of failures and hardships, to discover the source of the Nile. It took some six years before Henry Morton Stanley, a young and brazen correspondent for the New York Herald, tracked him to a village called Ujiji, and accosted him with that famous greeting "Doctor Livingstone, I presume"? Stanley had followed the Doctor's trail for three full years, braving disease, difficult terrain and all manner of deprivation before achieving his goal and emerging as one of the most famous explorers of the time. And this fame brought him to the attention of King Leopold II, who retained him as his official representative and prompted him to return to Africa to explore the Congo River watershed. And inasmuch as it was Stanley's success in locating Livingstone that brought him and the King together, Livingstone played a decisive role in the history of the Congo.

And now comes time to write about Stanley. However, since his early years in Africa were inexorably intertwined with Livingstone, they will both appear in following paragraphs.

The expedition financed by the New York Herald, with a total complement of 190 men, was the largest caravan ever assembled in Africa. It is obvious though that, despite its size, the expedition would have failed to reach Ujiji, had it not been for Stanley's strong leadership and unwavering determination (no wonder the natives called him Bula Matari, which means "Breaker of Rocks"). But reach Ujiji it did, and Stanley accomplished the mission that had been entrusted to him by the newspaper. He remained with Livingstone for months, before finally returning to Zanzibar with the Doctor's journals and a sealed packet of his letters. They were Livingstone's reports of his last journeys, and the incontestable proof that Stanley did indeed meet him in Ujiji.

Unfortunately, Livingstone did not live to see Zanzibar again. He had been in poor health for some time, and eventually died on the shore of Lake Bangwelu in 1873, still searching for the source of the Nile. His faithful native companions buried his heart alongside a tree, right where he had died, so that it would remain forever on African soil, on the very continent that captivated Livingstone for most of his adult life. They dried his body in the sun, and preserved it in salt before carrying it to Zanzibar in a coffin of bark. In due time, he was buried with great honors in London's Westminster Abbey, grieved by Stanley and hundreds of mourners who came to pay their respects to this great man.

Although Livingstone never located the actual source of the Nile, he nevertheless made a meaningful discovery around the mid 1800's. It was a place known by the natives as "Mosiloa-Tunya" (Thundering Smoke), which is an apt name for the area where the Zambezi River suddenly tumbles over a deep cliff. This cliff is about one mile long, but narrow enough to appear from the air as a mere fissure in the earth. The water plunges some 400 feet into the abyss of a dark gorge, striking the rocky floor with a deafening roar that is heard for miles around. The perpetual mist created by the crashing waters rises 1000 feet into the air, and accounts for the falls' well-known double rainbow. Dr. Livingstone named these majestic falls "Victoria Falls" in honor of Queen Victoria of England. By the way, this is where the Zambezi River forms the border between Zambia and Zimbabwe, the two countries previously known as Northern Rhodesia and Southern Rhodesia.

I happened to be around Victoria Falls a couple times in my life. The first time does not count for much because I remember seeing only the extraordinary "Thundering

Smoke" from the window of a train. The train had stopped briefly on the bridge over the Zambezi River, downstream from the falls, to let us glance at the famous scenery. It was in1945, and I was on my way to a boarding school in Cape Town, South Africa, a three-day train journey from Elisabethville. Well, the experience did not excite me very much, yet it made for a nice break in the boring monotony of the long journey. By the way, the bridge in question was built on the orders of Cecil Rhodes, English financier and diamond magnate, who dreamt of building a railroad line from Cape Town to Cairo.

My second visit, some ten years later, was quite a winner. I went there on vacation with my friends and colleagues from the Aero Club Royal du Congo Belge. We chartered a Sabena DC-4, and flew from Leopoldville to Livingstone in Zambia, where, after parking the plane at one end of the airport, we climbed into several cars for the drive to the Victoria Falls Hotel, in Zimbabwe. On the way, we went over the same bridge that my train had used in 1945, and, mere minutes after crossing the Zambezi River, checked into the hotel. This hotel was strategically located alongside the right-bank of the Zambezi River, and its immaculate grounds offered a panoramic view of the falls and the Batonga Gorge. And when dusk came and our dinner was over, the large patio overlooking the grounds became an excellent spot for drinks and a welcome relief from the sweltering heat inside the hotel (remember that this was prior to the advent of universal air conditioning). Even the high-pitched noise of the large locust, and the dining room's dress code demanding jacket and tie (this venerable British custom had to be respected no matter how hot it got) were unable to dampen our high-spirited gatherings during the long evenings.

We explored the falls and strolled through the miniature rain forest in the thick of the falls' mist. We went on boat trips among the enormous hippos, watched elephants roaming at the river's edge, went on a safari tour of the Wankie National Park and even had a picnic on an island teeming with baboons. Wildlife was really all around us. At times, monkeys and wart hogs would scamper on the back lawn of the hotel, and quite often we had to step over elephant dung when we walked from the hotel to the falls.

The bottom of the falls was reached in one of two ways - by walking or by using trolleys of the Rhodesian Railways. These were mere platforms set on rails, with open sides and only a canopy for a roof. Each was fitted with a couple of benches, one along each side, placed back-to-back, with enough room for six tourists. There were no engines on these contraptions. And though no power was needed to reach the bottom of the gorge, of course, something was needed to propel the trolleys back up the sheer cliff. And that something was what Africa had the most of; namely manpower. Employees of the Rhodesian Railways pushed the trolleys, at the sweat of their brows and to the recurrent beat of a happy tune, all the way to the top of the gorge.

Time flew by, and suddenly, our vacation was over and we were back inside our DC4, properly lined up on the runway for liftoff from Livingstone's airport. Once in the air, the pilot made a number of low-altitude passes over the falls before climbing to our proper altitude and heading back home. From the air, the scenery was riveting. The Zambezi River, about a mile wide at this point, approaches the falls by a gentle incline, before tumbling suddenly over the edge of the narrow chasm that is so characteristic of Victoria Falls. This chasm is the reason why one must get up really close to see the actual falls (unlike, for instance, Niagara Falls that can be admired from a reasonable distance). Finally, let me point out that the low supply of water during the dry season can leave the Zambian side of the falls absolutely dry from time to time. But during the rainy season the flow is immense. The Zambezi rises in northwest Zambia, with many of its headwaters flowing from the jungles of Angola. And that is why in the rainy season, which usually peaks around April, the river swells to the point that it can toss up to 17 million cubic feet of water per minute over the width of the falls.

Back now to the trilogy and Stanley, the man who became the King's point man in Africa and helped the Belgian Monarch capture the huge Congo River basin as his personal domain. Since it was Stanley's explorations that made it all happen, the next paragraph will cover the history of his life.

Sir Henry Morton Stanley (1841-1904) came from Wales. His real name was John Rowlands, but he took on the name of the cotton broker who hired him when he landed in New Orleans. He was almost eighteen at the time. He fought in the Civil War-on both sides of the conflict (showing early on his penchant for extreme adventures).

First he joined the Confederate Army, but that came to a sudden end when he was captured by the Federal Army, and confined temporarily to a prison camp. Upon release, he enlisted in the United States Navy, and sailed on the USS Ticonderoga. After the war, he became a foreign correspondent and, in 1869, the New York Herald gave him the enviable assignment of finding Dr. Livingstone, the task that eventually made him world famous.

A couple of years after his famous meeting with Dr. Livingstone, and his return from Africa, Stanley went back to the African continent to embark on the most ambitious and most hazardous journey of his career. Financed by the New York Herald and the London Daily Telegraph, he organized an expedition to cross the entire continent of Africa, from east to west. The journey was to start in Zanzibar, go to the infinite headwaters of the Congo and follow the river to its mouth on the Atlantic Coast. And once again, he achieved his goal. He was gone for two and a half years and covered a zigzag course of over 7,000 miles, before emerging at last from the interior. But this astounding achievement came at quite a cost. All three of his fellow Europeans, and 173 of the native carriers died before the survivors reached the Atlantic Coast in 1877.

Stanley returned to Europe to regain his health, and to make a first hand report to the world about his fabulous journey through the heart of the Dark Continent. But a year later, the King convinced him to go back to Africa as his personal representative, and to organize a new expedition to the river's basin. Back he went to plant the king's flag all along the route of his caravan and to open trade posts in the prime areas of the bush. He negotiated treaties in the name of the monarch with all the influential chiefs of the region.

This was the way that the Congo Free State was hewn out of Africa. However, Stanley eventually came to regret his involvement with the king, and he worked hard to distance himself from the monarch and the atrocities committed by his agents. By assisting the King in "colonizing" Western Africa, he had unwittingly helped create one of the most outrageously enslaved nations in history.

After Stanley stopped running expeditions in Africa, he came to live in London, became a naturalized citizen of Great Britain and was even elected to the British Parliament, where he served until 1900. He died of a stroke and pleurisy in 1904. And though the memorial service was held in Westminster Abbey, he was not buried next Livingstone, his friend and fellow explorer. The dean of Westminster Abbey refused to have him interred in the hallowed grounds of the cathedral because of his past association with King Leopold II, and slavery.

Stanley was buried in Pirbright's churchyard, some twenty-five miles outside London. His granite tombstone reads;

Henry Morton Stanley

Bula Matari

1841-1904

AFRICA

12. Elisabethville, The End of Our Trip

Dilolo, in the Belgian Congo, was a tiny fleck on the map, but it loomed rather large in our minds since it meant that we were finally reaching the end of our long journey. It was a small post with a nondescript administrative building where passengers were processed through customs and immigration. But, when our turn came to go through the formalities, it was found that our travel documents lacked a certain visa and, for a brief moment, our parents actually thought the family might be held at the border. In the end, everything worked out pretty well; we were allowed to proceed on our trip, and father was instructed to resolve the problem with the authorities in Elisabethville.

We had scarcely climbed on board when we heard the locomotive's whistle, and felt the train pull away from the platform. I guess we had been the very last passengers to come back on board, and the conductor had patiently waited for us before allowing the locomotive to move on. How many people can say that a whole train was held for them?

The landscape outside our compartment window did not change much at first. But what did change immediately was the language. The signs in all the small railroad stations that we sped through were now written in French. Also, the personnel on the train addressed us in French, instead of

Portuguese, and the Congolese Franc became the currency of the day. The stations that I mentioned looked clean, well maintained, and most of them had flower beds around platforms. Later on we found that this was the norm for railroad stations in the Congo.

Father had exchanged our Angolan funds for Congolese money, while we were in Dilolo, and we spent time familiarizing ourselves with the new currency. I liked the coins most of all. They had pictures of elephants and palm trees, and the ten centimes coin had a hole in the middle. The fifty centimes coin was engraved with the notation "Albert Roi des Belges" (Albert King of the Belgians- instead of King of Belgium). The explanation for this is quite simple; when Belgium became independent in 1830, it needed a monarch to head the government and, since the country had no royalty to draw from, Prince Leopold of Saxe-Coburg was elected by popular vote to become their King. He accepted this great honor and, hence, became the King of the Belgian People. That distinctive title continues to this day.

Now, while I was curious about the Congolese currency, I was also beginning to wonder about the value of my hoard of silver-foil wrappers (the one thing that my adventure books clearly proclaimed as the only "currency" readily accepted by most natives in Africa). I could no longer disregard the fact that, during our entire train journey, I had not seen a single native trade his goods for anything else but real white man's money, even though we had passed through some pretty remote areas at that. Did this mean that I was not going to be able to buy my chimp with all that silver-foil? And while on the subject of pets, I realized with foreboding that I had yet to see the first wild animal, even though I had already spent many days traveling through Africa. What was going on? Where was all that wildlife? I was getting discouraged and quite impatient. But I should not have worried. Not long after we reached Elisabethville, Harry and I became the proud owners of a wonderful monkey.

As our trip proceeded, we kept crossing innumerable rivers, all of them flowing north into the huge depression that makes up most of the country, the depression that is drained single-handedly by the powerful Congo River. Actually, we even crossed the Congo River itself. It happened a few miles after our brief stop in Kolwezi, a mining center for copper and other minerals, such as cobalt, uranium, etc. I have never visited the town, but Harry ended up living there for two years, and he told me all about it some time later. The copper is taken out of an immense open pit that extends almost to the center of town and generates the reddish dust that covers the whole town from top to bottom. The noise of the huge trucks that carry the ore out of the pit is inescapable, and is hard getting used to. Especially since the activity of the mine goes on around the clock.

The stretch of the Congo that we encountered outside Kolwezi is called the Lualaba River. Its source originates far to the south of town, close to the Angolan border, from where it goes straight north to Lake Mweru and, once it exits the lake, resumes its run to the Atlantic Ocean.

The only other large town that we stopped in was the town of Jadotville, a town only a few hours from Elisabethville, the end of our trip. My excitement became intense right then, and it required several trips to the lavatory before my nerves calmed down (my family is known for its nervous digestive system).

At last, the train reduced speed and pulled leisurely into Elisabethville's rail depot. WE HAD ARRIVED.

13. Monsieur Rypar

We stepped on the platform and were at once greeted by two Bata men who materialized out of the crowd, having come to meet us at the train. They spoke Czech, and that made me feel great. I was finally able to communicate with strangers without using hand gestures.

After some brief introductions, they assembled our luggage and led us from the depot to a couple of cars parked right outside the building. One car was loaded with our luggage, and the other with us. Father sat in front, next to Monsieur Rypar, while the rest of us took the back seat. I remember his name quite well because Monsieur Rypar became a very good family friend, and at one time even lived with us. Since I do not remember the name of the other gentleman, I will refer to him as Monsieur X.

After we took off, Monsieur Rypar explained that our new home was close to the center of town, and that our future school, as well as the Avenue de L'Etoile, the downtown commercial hub, were within easy walking distance of the house. He promised to take us around later on, and went on to say that he had instructed our "boy" (houseboys were always called that, it was not meant to be racist) to have lunch ready by noon. Yes, this boy could cook quite well, continued Monsieur Rypar, but it shall be up to

mother to teach him some Czech recipes (as he said that, I
seemed to notice that he licked his lips). Monsieur Rypar
was a bit portly, and appeared to love food very much. It also
was clear to me that he was a jovial type (that does come
with an extended girth, doesn't it?) and I knew at once that
we would get along pretty well. Anyway, he informed father
that the company paid for only one boy, and that wages for
additional servants, such as a laundry boy or a gardener,
had to be paid by us. But wages for domestic help were low
and, once we made our decision, he would assist us in hiring
the best possible individuals for the various jobs. And while
on the subject of boys, Monsieur Rypar warned that those
buggers (his word) usually attempted to take advantage of
the new expatriates' inexperience with Africa and its natives.
For instance, the laundry boy might appear one day with an
iron-burn on one of father's shirts, and humbly apologize
for the damage. If, as expected by him, we made the mistake
of letting him keep it for his own use (after all, it could
no longer be worn by father), we would find, before long,
that one of the shorts suddenly suffered a similar accident.
However, if the shirt was torn to pieces and the rags given to
the house boy for dusting and other uses, no other clothing
would ever be burned again, for as long as that particular
laundry boy would remain in our employ. Another ruse
they liked to test on newcomers was to trick them out of an
advance on future wages. This time they would pretend that
they had spent all the money from their last wages and had
no way of providing food for themselves and their families.
They would swear that they had not eaten for over a week.

Henri Diamant

Well, here all one had to do is to explain with a straight face that, not having eaten for such a long time, they must have become immune to the pangs of hunger and, therefore, no longer in need for an advance. The thing to learn from all this, is that one had to be on constant guard, but always fair, while dealing with employees, and remember, above all, that a gullible expatriate ran the risk of being unable to control workers and to function effectively in Africa.

The car pulled to a stop in front of a stucco villa with a hip red-tile roof and a front door framed by long side windows. Broad cement steps, each side anchored by a large concrete planter, led to the door, and gave the front of the house a distinctive character. It was set way back from the road, in the middle of a large tract of land.

We stepped out of the car and met "our" boy, who was, under the supervision of Monsieur X, in the process of moving our luggage inside the house. Walking through the door, I saw that I had just entered in the most beautiful home that I had ever lived in. The large rooms had unusually high ceilings and lots of windows. There was a living room with an attached dining room, a kitchen and three bedrooms. Oh yes, also a large bathroom. As an added bonus, Harry and I discovered in the back of the house an immense walled yard. In Europe we lived in apartments and had no yards to ourselves, and now we had one that could easily compete in size with almost any of the fields in Kravsko (I guess my super-active mind was again playing tricks on me). The yard had a tall termite mound on one side (we climbed to the very top the minute we saw it), and a "boyerie" at the very end of the property. This boyerie was a one-room brick dwelling, with an outside shower and a cooking area. The boy used it on the days that he worked late and did not want to go back to his home in the native neighborhood outside the European city.

Lunch consisted of a chicken broth, a ragout and fruits for dessert. The food was well prepared and, to the obvious pleasure of our boy, was eaten with real gusto. Mother attempted to compliment him about his cooking talent, but finally had to ask our guests to help her out. Language was going to be a real problem for the foreseeable future.

We moved to the living room to drink our coffee and to wait for the end of the siesta. Officially, all businesses closed at noon and reopend after 2 pm (and as the saying goes, only mad dogs and Englishmen roam the streets in the mid-day heat). It was decided that, after the siesta, Monsieur X would return to the Bata store, while Monsieur Rypar would go on assisting us with our most immediate needs. He was thinking about taking us past the school, the various shops, etc., and in general help us find our bearings around town. Then, in the evening, Monsieur X would return to our house, and we would all have dinner in one of their favorite restaurants (they were both single and rarely ate at home).

While my parents walked Monsieur X to the door, I worked up enough courage to ask Monsieur Rypar about my "problem", or should I say despair, with regards to the hoard of silver foil wrappers. Was I correct to worry that I may not be able to trade the wrappers for a chimp? Were my adventure books all wrong about the silver foil "currency"?

I just rattled on and on, and evidently Monsieur Rypar noticed how upset I was getting about this whole thing. So, he waited until I unloaded my aching heart and then talked to me in a very tactful way. Yes, he said, it is true that many people outside Africa believe that the natives trade their goods for silver foil. And he agreed that, just as I had experienced it myself, even some books allege the same thing. But, truth be told, this is not so (I think my heart actually stopped beating at this point), and trading was done in the interior of the country only with glass beads, trinkets, cooking pots, etc. However, he continued with a broad smile, while chimps are hard to get, regular monkeys are a dime a dozen, and he was going to get me one after checking with father. Well, my despair evaporated right then and there, and I thanked Monsieur Rypar from the bottom of my heart. After all, a monkey was a perfect substitute for a chimp, and I could hardly wait to get my hands on one of those exciting pets.

Since siesta time was not over, there was no point going to town as yet, and so we sat in the living room while Monsieur Rypar resumed his talk about life in the tropics. He also gave us much advice.

First, he mentioned that Elisabethville, the provincial capital of Katanga, is located on an elevated plateau and, as such, enjoys mildly tropical temperatures. It is sunny except, of course, during the dry season that lasts from May to September. Actually, he said, there are those who go so far as to equate the local weather with the warmer areas of the Mediterranean, such as the island of Rhodes. According to Monsieur Rypar, we could not have asked for a better introduction to Africa.

However, he continued, it is important to remember that this is still Africa, where one must sleep under a mosquito net, take a daily dose of quinine and never step into a full sun without wearing a sun helmet. Also, one must never put on an enclosed shoe before making absolutely sure that it does not harbor a scorpion, or any other such creature.

At that point he drank some cold beer and went on for a fairly long while.

The natives are respectful of whites and often become devoted servants (women, as a rule, do not work in town). Contacts between Europeans and Congolese are mostly work-related. The center of town is reserved for whites, while the natives live in communities called "Cites", all of them located outside the town limits. Each evening, all natives must return to their communities and only household workers are allowed in town after 9:00 pm, as long as they carry a note from their employers stating that they worked late and were unable to beat the curfew. Conversely, a white man was not allowed in a "Cite" after 9:00 pm, because the Belgian colonial system was founded on the premise of "separate, but equal". Since a native was not allowed in town at night, then a white man was not allowed in the "Cite" at night. Since a native was not allowed to vote in elections, neither was an expatriate who lived in the Congo, and so on. But each colonial power had its own way to rule overseas territories. For instance, the Portuguese colonies of Angola and Mozambique were governed on the principle of assimilation, and in the eyes of the law everyone had equal rights.Incidentally, inter-marriage was prevalent in the Portuguese colonies, while it was not tolerated in the Congo (however, that does not mean that white men in the Congo did not live occasionally with native women, especially in the deep interior).

After that came the subject of barter, and Monsieur Rypar looked sideways at me when he started to explain to father that one must always drive a hard bargain when dealing with a native vendor. For instance, he continued, let's say that you want to buy a pet for your boys, such as a monkey maybe (boy, that Monsieur Rypar was good), and a native happens to come by with a cute one and offers to let it go for 20 francs. Well, even though you may think that 20 francs is a good price, under no circumstances should you agree to it. On the contrary, you should offer 5 francs and start walking away. You will end up getting that nice pet for no more than 10 francs.

This matter of barter led to an important subject, namely the law that forbids individuals to deal in diamonds and gold. The authorities stop at nothing in this respect, and even instruct undercover policemen to roam around town and offer uncut diamonds and matchboxes full of gold to anyone foolish enough to buy them. Prosecution is always swift and the consequences rather harsh. The Government owns all the mineral deposits in the country and takes drastic measures to safeguard all that wealth. No individual has the right to the minerals underneath his land. It is easy to obtain thousands of acres of free land from the Government, as long as a good portion of it is made productive within five years. Only then is the new owner issued the actual deed, a deed valid only for the surface of the land, not the minerals that may lie underground.

Did we know that hot liquids are better for you in the tropics than cold ones? Hot liquids make you sweat, and as the sweat dries off the skin, it creates a feeling of coolness. And all the while that Monsieur Rypar was telling us about the advantages of hot liquids, he was visibly enjoying his second glass of ice-cold beer (I found, later on, that alcohol plays an important role in white man's Africa). By the way, he was drinking Primus, one of the local beers. Another local beer on the market was Simba, the native word for lion.

The last topic covered by Monsieur Rypar, witchcraft, made me think immediately of Tarzan and his struggle against the evil powers of witch doctors and sorcerers. Not surprisingly, I hung on his every word and tried to forget the heat that was making me sweat uncomfortably (if this was called "mildly tropical temperatures", I was beginning to wonder what the true tropical temperatures felt like).

According to what Monsieur Rypar went on to say, no culture is immune to superstition. All civilized people do irrational things, like throwing salt over their shoulders when they spill some of it by accident, objecting to walk under ladders, unwilling to live on the thirteenth floor, and so on (some of us even believe that charms have certain powers). But primitive tribes carry superstition to the utmost degree and are totally devoted to irrational fetishism. The witch doctors' influence is all-pervasive and deep-rooted because Africans believe that misfortune is always the result of some terrible curse, and that witch doctors are the only ones with the powers to defeat black magic with their charms and potions. A fetish is supposed to have magical powers, and can make wishes come true, such as protect the village or strike down an enemy. And a sorcerer, with the right fetish, can send a crocodile or a hippo to kill any man he chooses. Hence, he must be both respected and feared.

While some rites continue to be practiced by the tribes, such as those of puberty, excision, circumcision, initiation and marriage, others can no longer be carried out in the Congo. The rites forbidden by the authorities were savage and hideous, such as cannibalism. Cannibalism, which is the only crime in the Congo that carries the death penalty, is supposed to transfer a victim's unique power and knowledge to the cannibal. So, if speaking French is the objective, find a person that is fluent in the French language and have his brain for dinner. There could be no easier way to acquire knowledge, right?

It may seem that I am jumping ahead, once again, but I feel that, because superstition and witchcraft are being discussed, here is the perfect place to write about how much they influence the every-day lives of the natives. Actually, I saw this personally when I witnessed the terrible fear that struck our cook when he entered, for the very first time, the kitchen of our new house in Leopoldville.

This particular boy had trained in the Catholic mission of Lusambo, and had become quite a worthy cook. As a matter of fact, his French pastries were some of the best that we had ever eaten. And the admirable thing was that he performed his miracles while working in a most primitive kitchen, one with no running water or electricity, where all cooking was done on a wood stove. And so, when we left Lusambo, we convinced him to follow the family to our new home in the capital city of Leopoldville. We flew, of course, while he went the long way by river boat. When he finally arrived, and mother took him to our new kitchen with its customary appliances, such as an electric stove, a sink with running water, etc., he turned deathly pale and disappeared as fast as his feet would carry him. Once we caught up with him in the back of the yard, we learned that he had run away because he had seen water boiling in a pot that was merely resting on some kind of a counter. Obviously, this was the result of a very powerful witchcraft. How else could a kettle boil water without the help of fire? He was terrified, and his fear was very real. However, it did not take long before he became quite comfortable with those newfangled devices, and went on to delight us again with his wonderful cooking.

Returning to that first day in Elisabethville, I should mention that, while Monsieur Rypar talked about life in Africa, mother had the boy unpack our luggage, and managed to have everything stowed away before siesta came to an end. She used a lot of hand commands, and by the time the job was done, had developed a good communication system with the house boy.

Myself, Mom, and Harry.

The family circa 1939. Harry, father, mother,
and me on the swing.

The SS Leopoldville took us from Antwerp, Belgium, to
Loanda, Angola. The sailing took two weeks.

Here I am giving the bottle to my first pet monkey.

The Bata Store in Lusambo, Belgin Congo. We lived on the
second floor.

Myself, dad, and Harry standing in front of Sabena's Fokker
Wulfe parked on Lusambo's grassy strip.

Approach to Bata's factory compound on the Avenue de
L'Industrie in Leopoldville, Congo Belge. This picture was
taken in 1949.

Pirogues and fishing village on the Congo River, upstream
from Leopoldville.

Zora and I playing with a snake.

The famous Piper Super Cruiser and me. We are at the
N'Dolo Airport in Leopoldville, Belgian Congo.

Preparing for a local flight over Luanda, Angola, with the
manager of the Universo Hotel.

View of a portion of Victoria Falls, taken from the
Zimbabwean side.

Ready to go on one of my first Liberties.

Posing on the renowned Acropolis,
high above Athens, Greece.

Riding a bike on the beach of Rhodes.

Here I am strolling with Eliska downtown in Nice, France.

14. Life in Elisabethville

When siesta finally ended, we grabbed our sun helmets and walked down the front steps toward Monsieur Rypar's car. But, the minute we left the dim refuge of the house, it seemed as if we had stepped into an oven working at full blast, and we found ourselves struggling under the fierce tropical sun. The brightness of the rays was dazzling, so that we had to squint for a while, to get our eyes adjusted to the blazing light. Well, if this was what a "mild" tropical temperature felt like, I started to wonder once again what a "full-fledged" tropical climate was meant to be like.

As expected, the minute we entered the car and opened all four windows (many years later I heard that this is called the 4x60 air-conditioning; open 4 windows and drive 60 miles an hour), Monsieur Rypar resumed chatting about life in the Congo, and especially about Elisabethville, as follows:

The avenues, which were laid out around the 1900s, were wide and lined with a variety of trees (such as jacarandas, mangoes and, of course, palms). Also, he pointed out, most of the intersections were built with attractive roundabouts filled with an abundance of multi-colored flowers. The commercial center evolved initially around the Avenue de L'Etoile (Avenue of the Star). But eventually other avenues, such Avenues de Kasai, Moero and Sankuru acquired a variety of large stores, offices and financial institutions. However, the fancier retailers, the ones that catered to the particular needs of Europeans, were still located chiefly on the Avenue de L'Etoile (mother was shown where to shop for groceries, etc...).

The city expanded rapidly from the time the Union Miniere du Haut Katanga, a quasi-governmental mining entity formed in 1906, began to develop the gigantic Mine Etoile, or Star Mine (this obsession with the word "star", has something to do with the Free State's original flag which featured, as I mentioned earlier, a gold star on a dark blue field) in the town's immediate vicinity, where huge deposits of copper extended all the way to the surface of the dirt. The native miners who worked the mine, while forced to perform hard labor, profited greatly from their toil by living in small brick houses organized into neat native towns that had free schools and hospitals, roads, electricity and running water, luxuries that had never before been available to Africans in this corner of the world.

Children from European families were sent to whites-only schools. The boys attended the College Saint Francois de Sales, run by Salesian priests, and the girls were taught at the Institut Marie-Jose where nuns held sway (we are talking about catholic clergy in white vestments and, as Harry and I learned quickly enough, totally dedicated to the strictest of disciplines – such as full obedience at all times). These schools were conveniently located within an easy stroll from our new home, exactly as Monsieur Rypar had mentioned earlier. For that matter, even the town's swimming pool, called the Lido, happened to be relatively close. It was an Olympic-size pool, with cabanas and several clay tennis courts. Naturally, this was also a whites-only facility.

It did not take long to criss-cross the downtown area since it was relatively small and motorized traffic was light. It had a clean business center, attractive residential areas, manicured lawns and tons of greenery.

As one might expect though, a lot of time was spent that afternoon at the Bata Shoe Store and the new premises for Kotwa's future office. Father and Monsieur Rypar talked a lot about current business activities and the uncertainties of the situation back home. Should Hitler invade Czechoslovakia, Bata's overseas divisions shall be cut off from Zlin's production, financing and long-term directives, bringing about a critical disruption of business for the duration of hostilities. Hopefully, though, the world would dodge this crisis, and Bata's commerce in the Congo would continue to develop in line with the latest projections and estimates. Obviously, as true company-men, they could not bring themselves to consider the possibility of failure, no matter what underlying causes might come into play.

Then the discussion turned to commercial activities in the bush, and Monsieur Rypar explained that, as new railroad lines pushed through the heart of the country, young expatriates moved right along with them and proceeded to establish a pretty good trade with the natives. They dealt in a variety of miscellaneous goods, such as clothing, mirrors, cooking pans, candles, and salt (salt was much in demand because it does not occur naturally in the hinterland). With their profits they bought local products, such as palm oil, manioc and cotton, for resale in the urban areas that grew up along the railroads' tracks. However, while this trade became pretty lucrative, life in the interior was no picnic for the white man. It actually became a daily fight against elements, illness and isolation. Contacts with missionaries and other white colonials were few and far between. They had no comforts, not even those of the most rudimentary kind; and certainly no social distractions, newspapers, electricity or radio, and no news of the world at large for weeks on end. Household boys had to fetch wood, water and even provide bush-meat. No wonder that some of the whites ended up with black female companions.

When dinner time rolled around, we drove to the town's hotel to meet Monsieur X for cocktails and a well deserved meal (initially, we were going to get together back at our house, but that was changed because we had been delayed downtown). And though our meal dragged on late into the night, and I became very tired, I fully enjoyed that whole evening. I do not remember exactly what I ate, but I remember how memorable that dinner was, our first one in Elisabethville, in our brand new hometown.

During dinner, most of the discussion revolved around the next day's activities, and eventually the following schedule was set in place:

Monsieur Rypar would have breakfast at our house, and help mother work things out with our boy. His fluent French will come in handy to ease things along.

By eight o'clock, Harry and I will be taken to the

College Saint Francois de Sales, and begin the French phase of our education. Being the eternal optimist, I actually looked forward to all that, and started thinking about new friends and experiences. Harry, on the other hand, was apprehensive and did not appear happy about the next day's prospects.

Next, Monsieur Rypar will take our parents to Elisabethville's City Hall, to straighten out the matter of missing documents that the immigration authorities in Dilolo found lacking in our visas files, and to get the indispensable residential permits for the family.

Then, mother will be left at the grocery to do some marketing, while father and Monsieur Rypar will spend time in the office.

And that is exactly how things evolved that first full day in Elisabethville.

15. My First Monkey

In the following days, Harry and I easily adjusted to our unfamiliar surroundings. There was, of course, the heat and the need to wear sun helmets throughout the day. We had to take daily dosages of quinine and, to be safe from mosquito bites during the night, we slept under mosquito nets. To guard against nasty scorpions and other creepy creatures, we learned to check the inside of our shoes before getting dressed, and never to reach into holes, under rocks or other snug places without first making sure that no unfriendly critters had claimed them already for their own. In other words, we followed Monsieur Rypar's advice to the letter.

We also had to adapt to a life without fresh milk. Cattle were not raised in the area because of the tsetse flies that carry the nasty sleeping sickness, and because the local markets were not able to provide fresh milk from distant places. Thus, we became accustomed to a powdered-milk product called KLIM. Do you get it? It is the word "milk" spelled in reverse.

In school, we were both placed in the third grade, so that we could be taught French together. However, they did assign us to our respective grades, third for me and fifth for Harry, for all math courses. Anyway, part of the French lessons included reading a ton of comic books, and

I believe that this helped greatly with our struggle to learn the language. But those readings also resulted in another advantage, at least as far as I was concerned. I came upon the remarkable adventures of Tintin and Milou, his faithful dog - Tintin being an intrepid young reporter whose exploits took him to the farthest corners of the globe, and even outer space. These exceptional comic strips were printed with impressive graphic details and were full of lively characters that I readily identified with. Publishing was done under the nom-de-plume of Herge, who was really the Belgian writer Georges Remi. His success grew with each new story and, eventually, Tintin's adventures were translated into 77 languages. As for me, I became so thoroughly thrilled by the amazing exploits of those two heroes that, from time to time, I still enjoy perusing my prized collection of Tintin's wonderful adventure books.

Then came the dreadful day of Germany's invasion of Czechoslovakia. The date was March 15, 1939, some two weeks after we arrived in Elisabethville. That evening, our parents and Monsieur Rypar talked far into the night, long after Harry and I crawled under our mosquito nets.

Our parents told us, the minute we woke up the next morning, that Monsieur Rypar would be moving in with us. They explained that this was due to the tragic events in Czechoslovakia, and the uncertain future that was threatening the entire world (it was then that I remembered our parents and Monsieur Rypar discussing something of the kind during our first day in Elisabethville). The rationale for Monsieur Rypar's move was clear. Zlin might be prohibited

by the Nazis to finance its overseas' business activities and/
or to supply merchandise to branches outside of the Nazi
area of influence. When Austria was annexed, they had
taken instant and total control of all major Austrian banks
and industries, and so, the same course of action should be
expected in Czechoslovakia. As a result, there was only one
thing to do, and that was to eliminate immediately as many
expenses as possible. And the one expense that came to mind
at first, was the high rent the company was paying for each
of its employees' villas. Thus, it was decided that Monsieur
Rypar would give up his villa, and move to the empty
bedroom in our house. And that, as far as I was concerned,
was the greatest news of the moment, no matter what the
reason. I was not old enough to really grasp what this was all
about.

My first impression of Monsieur Rypar, at the time
we stepped off our train in Elisabethville, proved correct.
He was definitely jovial and great fun to be with, and
immediately insisted on being called by his first name
of Jenda. And this shows the caliber of the man when
you consider that some Belgian children were still using
the deferential French pronoun "vous" (you) instead of
the intimate "tu" (thou), when addressing their very own
parents. And they certainly would not, customarily, address
adults by their first names.

Jenda was also as good as his word, and it was not long
before he really came through for me in a big way. He
had not forgotten our discussion about pet monkeys and
wasted little time to make good on his promise. One day,

as we arrived home from school, we found a baby monkey waiting for us under one of the big trees in the backyard. Jenda had seen a street vendor carrying it down the road, callously crammed into a small rattan cage, and decided to buy it for us right then and there. It needed affection and nourishment. We gave it both at once and without restraints. Mother provided us with a baby bottle full of milk and some vital instructions. Feeding became a team effort, while one of us hugged the tiny creature against his chest, the other worked the bottle.

This was absolutely the most beautiful pet I had ever seen. The small body was covered with thin fluffy grayish hair, and was topped by a round head featuring huge sad eyes and tiny ears. Its tail was long and thin. It kept hugging us whenever we picked it up and, before long, its eyes lost their sadness and it turned into a very playful and happy pet. It was the source of much fun and great enjoyment for the entire family.

During the day it remained tied to a nice shelter, something like a doghouse, that Harry and I built out of a wooden crate from father's office (in those days, goods were transported in wooden crates, not cardboard boxes). But once we got home from school, we let it romp free in the yard and play with us. It never attempted to run away.

Oh sure, once in a while it turned into quite a pest. Such as when our vegetable garden, lovingly nurtured by Harry and me, started to yield tasty results. It would scamper into the garden, pick some of the juiciest vegetables, and run up a tree before we could do anything about it. So, we had to keep it tied down around "harvest" time, especially when the cucumbers started to mature. They were really good, and the whole family enjoyed them thoroughly, including Jenda. Some forty years later, I received a letter from him where he reminisced about old times, and actually mentioned these famous cucumbers. The letter came from the French Riviera, where he had retired with his wife Petruska, after they had left the Congo for the final time in the late 1980's. Petruska used to live next door in Elisabethville, and Jenda met her when he came to live with us (he gave her that lovely Czech name when they became an "item", and it stuck to her for good). She was a charming and beautiful South African lady of British origin, who worked for a large car agency in town. They had no children, other than their dogs. Petruska's baby was a chihuahua, while Jenda's buddy was a bulldog- the contrast between those dogs was hilarious.

We spent a lot of our free time, Harry and I, in our yard. There was no end to the action-packed adventures that we were able to enact among the termite mound and large trees. We let our imagination run wild and went for it. But in the end, I think that our greatest undertaking was the vegetable garden, and we worked hard and long to make it our pride and joy.

There is also a story about a small child who lived several houses down the street, in a villa with another oversized yard. He was a very poor eater, no matter what his mother did to try to improve his appetite. So, imagine how delighted she became when this situation perked up all of a sudden, and she had to be swift with preparing his morning bottle. He would grab it as soon as it was ready and rush outside, to return some time later with a bone dry bottle. This went on for several days until the mother, with her uncanny motherly instinct, realized that something was amiss. She followed him the next time he went out, and froze in her tracks. Her son was petting a large snake, while the reptile was happily sucking on the nipple. The two had become good friends, and were helping each other in their own ways.

The whole episode seems unreal, but I remember it vividly and, although Harry has no recollection of it, I am convinced that it happened just the way I described it.

Another event that I remember quite vividly, and have the scar to prove it, is the one that happened just before our mid-term vacation, on the last day of school. I was riding home on my bike, happily chanting over and over "vive les vacances, plus de penitence, les cahiers au feu et le prof au milieu" (hurrah for the holidays, no more punishments, notebooks into the fire and the teacher right in the middle). I was not paying attention to the road, so I was not ready when the front wheel hit some very deep sand and the bike stopped dead in its tracks. Unfortunately, I was rolling rather fast at the time and, as the bike came to an abrupt halt, I flew right over the handlebar. That, by itself, would have been bad enough. But, the incident took a turn for the worse because of a ruler that I had wedged in the handlebar to anchor the straps of my satchel. This darn ruler tore into my right knee and made a cut some three inches long from side to side. I managed to limp home with the help of Harry, and was rushed to a doctor. Well, I still think of him as a butcher, not a doctor. A couple of his male nurses pinned me down while he worked on my knee, without deadening the area or giving me medication against pain. That was not an auspicious start for a vacation, but as the saying goes, that is how the cookie crumbles. Just think, had this happened during the school year, I would have earned myself a few days of freedom, and would have gained something from all that pain and suffering.

Finally, I want to mention the wonderful fables, written by La Fontaine, that we read and studied in class. Jean de La Fontaine was a French poet who lived in the 1600's and who wrote pointed stories about animals and nature, much like those composed by Aesop (some people feel that he drew inspiration and actual material right out of Aesop's writings). I was engrossed by those fables, and can still remember quite a bit of "The crow and the fox" (Le corbeau et le renard). The story centers about a crow high up a tree, holding a cheese in its beak. A fox, tempted by the cheese's aroma, flatters the crow by telling him how beautiful he is and that, should his voice match his looks, he would clearly reign as the supreme creature of these woods. Well, the fox won the cheese and the crow learned, a bit late, that all flatterers live at the expense of those who listen to them.

16. The Dark Days

Month followed month, and the situation in Europe became gloomier and gloomier. After the invasion of Czechoslovakia, the Germans divided the country into the Protectorates of Bohemia and Moravia, and allowed Slovakia to declare independence. It became the Republic of Slovakia, and allied itself immediately with the Nazis. But because the Congo was insulated from Europe, it was weeks before we learned of this development.

Fortunately, Zlin had decided, well ahead of the invasion, to rush out of the country substantial consignments of all types of footwear. Some of these shipments eventually reached Elisabethville, and ultimately filled the local warehouse to the brim. This relieved Jenda's anxiety about the retail division's short-term future, but it did nothing to ease father's concerns. Kotva was an Import Agency and, as such, shipped   goods to volume customers directly from overseas' factories, not a local warehouse. Kotva's future looked gloomy indeed.

Then came the catastrophic events that, forever, affected the entire planet and all humanity. Hitler's forces slammed into Poland on September 1, 1939, and World War II erupted on September 9, 1939. International trade and travel were drastically disrupted. Congo became more isolated than ever before.

Hitler continued his conquests and, on May 10, 1940, German troops attacked Belgium. The Belgians did their best to resist the invading enemy, but after eighteen agonizing days, King Leopold III decided to capitulate and, in doing so, save many thousands of military and civilian lives. The capitulation was ratified on May 28, 1940, and German troops quickly moved all over the country, invading Belgium for the second time in the twentieth Century.

This tragic situation led to a critical period for the Congo. Governor General Ryckmans proclaimed that the Colony would go on fighting for the liberation of the homeland, and ordered the arrest of all German and Italian nationals, except their missionaries. German and Italian Jews were also incarcerated, but only for a very short time. It took a couple of weeks before the authorities realized the irony of the situation (by then, alarming rumors had already circulated about the fate of Jews in Nazi-occupied areas), and released unconditionally all foreign residents of Jewish extraction.

Congo's support of the war effort became vital. Huge quantities of copper, manganese, cobalt, and industrial diamonds were supplied regularly to the Allies' industrial centers. Also, as I already mentioned, it was Congo's uranium that was used for the development and construction of the first atomic bombs. And, when the German North Africa Corp threatened El Alamein and Tobruck, the combined Belgian/Congolese Expeditionary Corp took part in the effort that tossed the North Africa Corps into the Sea.

During those dark days, while the adults were agonizing about the war and the safety of loved ones back home, Harry and I were enjoying a great time. We had broken through the language hurdle and felt completely in sync with our new lives. Day in and day out, we wore shorts, short-sleeve shirts and open sandals. We swam almost daily at the Lido and learned to play tennis. School was pretty easy, except that we were always loaded with homework by teachers that were quite responsive to students' needs, but altogether (in my opinion) unreasonably strict. There was no compromise on discipline, and punishment was harsh. But I quickly learned how far I could stretch the "ropes", and still remain out of trouble. The other thing that I learned fairly fast, was to keep my bare limbs well inside the bed's mosquito enclosure. Whenever any part of my body would so much as brush accidentally against the surface, it would be set upon by hoards of nasty mosquitoes that had been patiently waiting for their midnight meal.

Then, the inevitable happened toward the end of 1940. The Kotva division ceased to exist. In the beginning, father managed to generate enough income by selling off the entire inventory of samples to the general public. A large portion of this inventory consisted of furniture made of tubular steel, birch wood and chairs with caned seats. It was pure 1930's furniture, light and perfectly suited for the tropics. Under normal circumstances, this particular line of furniture would have become a huge success for Kotva. But, unfortunately, this was not to be. Anyway, father even dealt for a while in bales of used clothing that he obtained from a local merchant. But eventually, that merchandise dried up as well, and Kotva had to close its doors.

On the other hand, the footwear side of the company's business kept on going strong for two good reasons. Bata had monopolized the market with its reliable and well-priced merchandise, and the company's factory in Limuru, Kenya, was able to re-supply the stores periodically.

Thus, once Kotva was dissolved, father was transferred to the retail division.

And that became the scenario for yet another move for the four of us. The new destination was the village of Lusambo, a small outpost on the banks of the Sankuru River, in the Province of Kasai. It is located almost in the center of the country, right in the middle of its deep interior.

17. Moving to Lusambo

As far as I was concerned, the most difficult part of moving away was saying goodbye to my pet monkey. We had become good buddies and I did not want to leave it behind. But the anticipation of a life in the bush, instead of one in an urban environment, made my creative powers toil overtime. The notion of being able to see all kinds of wonderful animals, and the thought of living among them like a modern-day Tarzan eased the burden of giving up my very first monkey. Also, Petruska and Jenda decided to keep it themselves, which helped a great deal since I knew that they would take good care of it. But, saying goodbye to those two was also hard because I had become very fond of them both. However, less than a couple of years later, we became neighbors again, this time in the Bata compound in Leopoldville.

I am convinced that these types of experiences helped me mature into an optimist. To this day I still notice that the glass is half full, not half empty. I also believe that a silver lining can be found almost anywhere, no matter how foreboding a matter may seem at first.

When it was time to leave, Jenda took us to the railroad station and helped us settle down in our compartment before the train departed. It was a long journey to the northern town of Port-Francqui, on the banks of the Kasai River. The tracks from Elisabethville end there, so that goods and passengers have to use riverboats to continue on to Leopoldville via the Kasai and Congo Rivers.

We rolled northwest at first, over the very same tracks that brought us originally to Elisabethville. Then, about half way between Jadotville and Kolwezi, the train branched off and went due north, as if aiming straight for the Equator. We were going to leave it in the town of Luluabourg, where we were scheduled to take the road to Lusambo. It took some 48 hours to reach Luluabourg from Elisabethville.

On the way north, we stopped at a multitude of places, until they all ended up looking alike. But for some unknown reason, one stayed impressed in my mind, the town of Bukama, in the vicinity of the Parc National de L'Upemba, known for its lakes and large swamps. It is located on the right-hand bank of the Lualaba River. I remember also the ever-increasing heat and humidity. As we descended from the higher elevations and moved closer to the Equator, the average temperature and humidity kept going up and up, until we found ourselves sweating through our clothes and feeling clammy all day long.

We finally arrived in Luluabourg, and promptly boarded a rickety bus for the last leg of our trip. We were hot and tired, and eagerly looked forward to the journey's end. After all, we had to cover less than 200 miles to get to Lusambo, and that is not much of a stretch, right? Perhaps, but not really when one happens to travel in central Africa. Actually, it took eight hours of lurching and careening, on the poorest excuse of a road that I had ever seen in my life, to reach our destination. In some places the entire surface of the road was covered in an expanse of mud, and the bus bogged down whenever its wheels sank into the heavy muck. At that point, we would step out and wait on the side of the road until the native passengers pushed our vehicle out of the deep rut. Though this was typical for road-travel during the rainy season, it would not have been any better in the dry one. Then the bus would have lost traction in deep sand, and the result would have been the same.

Where rivers were wide and the current was strong, crossings were made on primitive ferries propelled along by a dozen natives with poles and paddles. Otherwise we merely drove into the water and forded over to the other side. Bridges were few and far between. And they were in terrible shape. At times they were so unstable that we were told to get off the bus and rejoin it only after it had crossed over to the other side.

Once in a while, we approached little villages of thatched mud-huts nestled around clearings overrun with chickens and children of all sizes. These kids, utterly naked, would stop playing their games and come running after the bus as it rattled past the village. The older natives would wave or bow respectfully.

As the day progressed, we experienced what I can define as the most oppressive and humid weather on earth. I fell into an Equatorial torpor, only to be rudely awakened by a loud thunderbolt. The sky had turned pitch-black and the temperature had become even more sultry and suffocating than earlier in the day. However, as the rain came down in heavy streaks and pummeled the bus, the air cooled off some, and breathing became easier. The thunderstorm broke within half an hour, and the sun reappeared in full force.

As we wound through some jungle for part of the day, I suddenly forgot all my discomforts and hardships. The forest crowded both sides of the road in a profusion of palms, tall trees and dense groves of bamboo. Sweeping ferns and hanging vines were everywhere. At times it appeared as if we were traveling through a dark tunnel. The vast canopy was so dense that sunlight was unable to penetrate through the intertwined branches. Other times, it looked as if we were rolling through canyons shaped by immense trees. Once, a monkey foraging on the side of the road, became frightened by our sudden presence, and ran immediately into the forest.

I was entranced by this wilderness. It looked just as I had pictured it when I first heard that we were moving to Africa. But, where were the animals? Except for that one monkey, we had seen nothing else during the day. We did not even see a single crocodile, despite all the rivers that we had crossed thus far. And while I was mulling over this inconceivable lack of animals, I suddenly observed a large flock of birds landing on some trees way ahead of us.

As we got closer to the flock, I heard a raucous noise full of squawks and squeals, and I realized that we had come upon a bunch of parrots. They were grey, with red tails, and they looked stunning. I had just set my eyes on the African Grey, the greatest speaking parrot in the world. And the more that I watched them, the more I wanted to get one of them for a pet. I could teach him to talk and do all kinds of tricks. I could carry him on my shoulders and make believe that I was a pirate. The possibilities were unlimited. I had to have a parrot as one of my next pets.

I must have fallen asleep again because the next thing I remember is mother telling me that we were nearing Lusambo.

18. Lusambo and the Sankuru River

The bus stopped on the bank of the Sankuru River, and we rushed out to stretch our limbs and get a glimpse of the town, which was hardly visible across the far side of the river's expanse. As we watched the old flatbed ferry move in to pick us up, we could not help but wonder what kind of life awaited us across the river. Little did we realize that we were about to begin the most unsophisticated and unaffected period of our existence. An existence devoid of the modern "necessities" and luxuries that we had taken for granted up to then.

Lusambo was an important strategic post that had been set up in the nineteenth century to prevent the Arabs from moving farther west and expanding their slave trade along the Atlantic coast. Its fortified camp, with a large detachment of the Free State's Force Publique (which eventually became, if you recall, Congo's Home Guard), played a pivotal role in the fight against these traders and their ultimate retreat from the territory. The primary campaign, which lasted from 1892 to 1894, resulted in the interception of many slave caravans and the liberation of large numbers of captives. But the fighting went on until 1901/02, and it was only then that the Arab slave traders were finally put down for good.

This post, which eventually became the seat of

government for the Province of Kasai (renamed later the Province of Kasai-Oriental), had an airport of sorts, a rudimentary hospital, a post office and a permanent garrison of the Force Publique.

The airport consisted of a grass strip with a small shed for odds and ends. A windsock was the only equipment at the facility. And to make matters worse, one end of the short runway was obstructed by a hill, while the river did the same on the opposite side. So, the planes had to taxi up to the hill, lock the brakes, rev up the engines as fast as they would go and, after releasing the brakes, accelerate toward the river and takeoff. The weekly arrival of Sabena's three-engine Fokker Wulfes became a social event.

Most of the white population came to the field to meet the arriving plane, and get first hand news of the outside world. Then, everyone would accompany the crew to the hotel for cocktails and dinner. The next morning, we went back to the field to say adieu to anyone leaving town, and to watch the plane takeoff. Once the passengers were on board, the ground crew inserted some kind of cartridge in each engine's starter, and pulled the trigger. The power of the explosion rotated the massive engines through a couple of revolutions and achieved ignition, without the need of starters and batteries.

Once the plane disappeared from view, we would go to the Post Office to pick up the mail that had been flown in the day before. Every family had a key to one of the mailboxes on the front wall of the small post office, and one could hear easily when something was pushed into it through the back. That was the clue to open the box and claim the eagerly awaited mail.

The Force Publique was the only military entity in the Congo. All the commissioned officers came from Belgium, as did most of the sergeants. Discipline was harsh and enforced, more often than not, with the "chicotte", a whip used liberally throughout the colony. And though the garrison in Lusambo was rather small, it was good at maintaining public safety, such as when the natives from across the river rebelled, and decided to visit their wrath on the white population. They were bold and brazen because they drank a lot of palm wine, and their witchdoctor's magical incantations promised them full protection against the white man's bullets. They took to their pirogues with machetes and spears, and were almost half way across the river before the Force Publique officer ordered his men to fire warning volleys over their heads. He thought that this would scare them off and stop the rebellion in its tracks. Unfortunately, it had the opposite effect. When the firing stopped and the warriors noticed that none of them had been hit, they concluded that the witchdoctor's power was indeed invincible, and that victory was in their grasp. Only dreadful carnage stopped them at that point.

The center of Lusambo had white stucco villas with large yards, most of them surrounded by whitewashed walls. These were the homes of about 200 Europeans, including their children, and groups of various missionaries. As was the custom, the natives, about 30,000, lived in surrounding villages. The few streets, and the road that crossed the town (all of them unpaved, of course), were lined with tall coconut palm trees that had been whitewashed on the lower portions of the trunks (I still do not know why whitewashing was so prevalent). The coconuts were harvested by inmates from the local prison, and given to the white residents in town. The prisoners climbed with bare feet and ran up and down the trees with only the help of a rope that stretched loosely around the trunks and their backs. I have yet to see anyone else climb as fast and as expertly as they were able to do it.

When we arrived in Lusambo, it had no running water, electricity or phones. The easiest luxury to live without was the telephone. Communicating around town was easily achieved with the use of personal messengers. Of course, the natives used tam-tams (drums) to communicate between villages, a system known as the "bush telegraph". I remember a friend telling us about his experience with this primitive, but effective, system of messaging. He had been on an inspection tour in the deep interior when, after a very long trek, he reached a remote mission without having first dispatched a runner to inform them about his impending arrival. But, as he started to apologize for dropping in unexpectedly, he was surprised to learn that the tam-tams had revealed his presence well in advance, and had even given the size of the expedition. These "talking drums" could be heard over many miles, and though different tribes had different modes of messaging, there seemed to be some universal method running through all the codes, so that each tribe understood what was being transmitted across the jungle. A talking drum is fashioned out of a hollow trunk, whose particular wood gives resounding sounds.

While on the subject of travel, I must point out that whites trekking in the interior usually stayed at Guesthouses maintained by the government in strategically located villages. These were large thatched huts that were looked after by a couple of natives, who also did the cooking and other chores for the traveler, all for a very nominal fee. The traveler just had to bring his own food, though.

Many nights, while I sweated under my mosquito net and listened to the drumbeats, I fantasized about being able to understand, one day, the mysterious messages that floated in the air, just like Tarzan. But thinking back, I now remember that, deep in my mind, I believed that there was a dark side to all the drumbeats pulsing through the night, a dark side that actually frightened me more than anything else. It was more scary than a sudden confrontation with a wild beast in the bush, or the vision of a snake curled up in my bed. What distressed me was the possibility that the drumbeats were reporting a rise of hostilities between warring tribes, or maybe the beginning of an assault on white people. I could handle the thought of wrestling with a lion, but not the notion of a throng of savages running through town with spears and machetes at the ready.

Drums were also used for rituals and ceremonies. They came in all types and sizes, and each village had a good variety of them on hand. During the day, they were placed in circles around open fires, so that the intense heat would stretch the hide of the drumheads tightly across the rims and get them properly primed for the evening's festivities.

The natives in our district were the Mongos, a part of the Tetela group, who shared Tchiluba for a common language. Endemic fever, strain-resistant malaria and sleeping sickness were prevalent in the area. The pagans among the natives (those not yet influenced by the missionaries), were devoted to a rude fetichism and lived in the most extreme of primitive states (cannibalism used to be common among some of the region's tribes). But no matter how primitive or civilized a tribe was at the time, all marriages followed the same age-old ritual. The potential groom had to negotiate with the father for his daughter's hand. It was only after they agreed on the number of goats, chickens and other valuables, that the ceremony could take place. And more often than not, this meant that the couple started married life in debt, something the missionaries tried to prevent. So they convinced several well-educated fathers not to extract payments from the grooms, and allow their daughters to marry in a religious ceremony. And though at first glance this appeared to be the right approach, it actually turned into a terrible mistake, and created problems between the couples. The new brides flatly refused to obey their husbands because they had not been purchased from their fathers. But in the end, it all turned out quite well. The husbands rushed to pay the fathers-in-law, and the brides immediately turned into loving and submissive wives. Their submissiveness was all encompassing, even to the point of always walking a few paces behind their husbands, and carrying back home, on their heads, anything the two purchased during their stroll. Husbands never carried anything.

Another significant issue is the natives' allegiance to family ties. It is a custom that dates from an old African morality principle that requires a person to help a relative in need, even if the family connection is a distant one. This same morality emphasizes tribal identity and imposes complete obedience to the village chief. The tribes are autonomous and often fight relentlessly among themselves, so that the whole country is usually awash with tribal tensions. Of course, this plays very nicely into the hands of the colonial authorities since policemen recruited from one tribe can always be trusted to maintain order between members of another tribe. Of course, this also works the other way round. Should the police revolt, the civilian population can be counted on to stay on the side and not come to the support of the policemen through riots or public disturbances. The powers that be developed this system to the umpteenth degree, and always put into practice the proven principle of "divide and conquer".

The Bas-Congo region endures a torrid and humid climate, and the area surrounding Lusambo has marshy areas, savannas overgrown with elephant grass and large zones of lowland forests. Coffee and cotton used to grow wild before large plantations were established on the riverbank opposite the town. Actually in some of these plantations, a few crumbling towers were still standing by the time we arrived. These were relics from times gone by, originally called "Boss Towers" (Tours de Maitre), used by white foremen to keep an eye on workers in the field, and single out those who had to be whipped at the end of the day.

The heat is at its worst, as expected, between noon and two, when everyone lapses into torpor and almost all activity comes to a standstill. This is the omnipresent daily siesta. The region has no evenings to talk about, a characteristic of the equatorial latitude. The red-hot sun drops swiftly behind the horizon at six in the evening, and then rises as quickly at six the following morning. The sunsets, in particular, are without equal anywhere else on earth. But daybreaks are also remarkable. Like magic, the tip of the sun emerges suddenly over the horizon, rising inch by inch, and in a matter of minutes transitions into a huge red fireball that glides effortlessly over the vast African sky. Nights are either pitch-black, or luminescent to the point of making it easy to see far into the distance.

At the onset of the rainy season, we looked for the inevitable pattern in the daily downpours. Within days this pattern became so reliable that we could practically set our watches by the start of the afternoon drenchers. The clouds would build up quickly and, amid bolts of lightning and great resounding clashes of thunder, rain would suddenly flood the land. Many of those storms were fearsome and the accompanying cracks of lightning were blinding. Really, no one could remain indifferent to the acrid odor of burned air when lightning struck in the immediate vicinity. I remember the time it hit entirely too close for comfort. It burst through a front window, flashed through the whole width of our house and flew out through one of the back windows.

Fortunately, no one got hurt, and the only damage was a cracked mirror that mother happened to be holding when the unwelcome visitor decided to pay us a visit. She was not injured, but it took an eternity before she and everyone else got their breath back. The lightning also ruined the two window screens that were in its path.

Now, before concluding my account about Lusambo's surroundings, and talking about the Sankuru River, let me say that the Bas-Congo region holds large deposits of diamonds, and that some of these deposits actually lay close to the very surface of the ground. Of course, this made the administration rather paranoid about illegal mining and resulted in firm controls on the commerce of uncut diamonds.

The Sankuru River, which is joined by the Lubi River south of Lusambo, is the longest tributary of the Kasai River which, in turn, joins the Congo River at a place called Kwamouth, some 150 miles east of Leopoldville. These navigable waterways, together with the Congo River, provide the ultimate route (the only practical route really) for the movement of goods from Lusambo and the Bas-Congo region, up to Leopoldville and overseas. The Sankuru River tends to be from half a mile to a mile wide and, though quite deep, has a moderate current, few islands and its banks are covered with forests up to the water's edge. The substantial depth, leisurely current and few islands, make it easily one of the safest rivers for paddleboats. Across the river from Lusambo, where the plantations thrived, the colonial administration maintained a large factory where cotton, the only commodity traded exclusively by the government, was processed into bales and taken to world markets by the riverboats that plied the Sankuru River. Harry became friendly with one of the captains, and he often allowed us to come on board to explore his boat. These boats had four or five cabins for the exclusive use of Europeans. The native passengers had to camp on the open decks, and cook their own meals with supplies brought along for the trip. They acquired additional foodstuff from peddlers who met the passing boats with pirogues full of food items at cheap prices.

19. Life in Lusambo

Abruptly the ferry cut its engine as it neared our side
of the river, and gently glided up to the landing area in one
even maneuver. It docked and was hardly tied down before
the ramp was dragged into place by a couple of deck-hands,
who tried to turn the craft around as fast as possible. Speed
was essential because dusk was drawing near and the ferry
could not operate in the dark.

Once we were on the other side of the river, Monsieur
Dvorsky, who knew father from Czechoslovakia, welcomed
us to Lusambo. They knew each other from the time when
Dvorsky was a salesman in one of the stores supervised by
father while he was the district manager for the Znojmo
region. He was intelligent and hard working, so father
enrolled him in one of the company's training programs
for managers, and helped him on the way to a promising
career. Needless to say, he was very friendly, and he did all he
could to help us cope with the primitive environment that
we had landed in. Later, when the time came to accompany
him to the airport, and see him off to his new assignment at
the company's headquarters in Leopoldville, he gave each
one of us, Harry and me, a gift that looked, at first glance
like a dispenser full of Gillette razor blades. We felt a little
crushed, and thought that this was some kind of a joke. But

when we opened our gifts, we discovered that each one held the fantastic sum of 100 Fr, a real fortune as far as I was concerned (that was the equivalent of $2.00).

Our new home turned out to be the second floor apartment over the Bata's Store. The two-story white stucco building, set on a corner lot, had a huge yard enclosed by a high whitewashed wall, and a corrugated-metal roof. The apartment was reached by an outside stairway that was built across the whole breadth of the left side of the building. It was truly a grandiose piece of architecture, with two individual flights of steps that led, from opposite sides of each other, to a wide landing midway to the top. From there, a single set of broad steps went the rest of the way to the final landing and the veranda's entrance. This was a wide wrap-around veranda that kept the sun's hot rays from the oversized windows and provided a vast area for lounging in open air. The windows had mosquito netting and louvered shutters, but no glass panes, so that the slightest breeze was able to cross-ventilate the apartment and keep us a little more comfortable in the torrid heat.

Part of the veranda doubled as a primitive bathroom facility. And when I say primitive, I really mean it in the pure sense of the word. It consisted of a crude cement tub that was set in an isolated corner, where it was possible to take a bath with a modicum of privacy. The water, hauled by one of our boys, came from the town's springs. Warm water, when needed, came from an old metal drum that stood in the yard, on a metal rack, and under which the gardener maintained a roaring fire.

In addition to providing hot water, the yard also fulfilled another essential need for the family. It held the household's trusty outhouse, at some distance from the house, right against one of the surrounding walls. It was cleaned out weekly by groups of convicts dressed in striped prison garbs, and shackled together by chains padlocked to thick metal rings fastened around their necks. The police guards wore blue shorts and shirts, and red fezzes on their heads. The details went from backyard to backyard and emptied the odorous contents into large containers fastened to bamboo poles carried on the men's shoulders. These men were prisoners that had been given harsh sentences, unlike the prisoners who harvested the coconuts around town.

Not far from our building, the town held two small shops that traded only in the most essential of necessities, a hotel and a guesthouse. That was the whole extent of the community's commercial establishments. The town had none of the shops and services that one would expect in an urban area, such as butchers, grocers, garages, dentists, pharmacists, et cetera.

The garrison of the Force Publique was located across the street from us, while the school and swimming pool were a little farther down the road, past the regional hospital. It was during our daily walks to and from school that we witnessed bodies being taken out for burial and saw gravely ill patients being brought in on primitive stretchers of woven mats and bamboo poles. Some appeared on the verge of death, not only because of what ailed them, but because they had been dragged over jungle trails for several days before getting to the hospital. I still remember vividly the ones who suffered from grotesquely swollen limbs, due to the ravages of elephantiasis. Typically, the hospital grounds had a bungalow, with four beds, reserved exclusively for the treatment of Europeans.

The hotel was extremely popular, not only because of the nice times that every one had there, but because it also doubled as the town's movie house. Of course, it did not have a real theater or even electricity. But, nonetheless, movies were shown every weekend.

This was the actual set-up:

Each Saturday morning, the hotel's messengers went around town with a note detailing the day's movie (this note had to be signed by every household because the hotel wanted proof that the messengers did as they were told). Later on that day, we would instruct our boy to take some of our chairs to the hotel's veranda and set them up for the evening's presentation. The veranda was large enough to hold the entire white population of Lusambo, with tables for drinks and food. Everyone tried to get to the hotel way before the start of the movie, so they would have time for drinks and friendly socializing with fellow expatriates. This intermingling was vital since people thrown together in the artificial closeness of expatriates' lives hunger for any kind of meaningful companionship. Another underlying reason was the fact that kinship was not really conceivable with the local population, due to the fundamental disparity that kept most Europeans and natives at arm's length.

The film was projected from the back of a truck that

used the electric power from its portable generator. It was parked against one end of the veranda, while the movie screen, consisting of a mere white sheet, was stretched at the opposite end. Well, that worked well unless something dreadful occurred, such as a cursed storm. To the deep disappointment of all, the operator would stop the film right then, and quickly put away his equipment until the following evening. That was when we would gather again on the veranda to watch what was left of the story. However, if another storm came around at the wrong time, we would never see the end of the movie because the truck (I should label it for what it was; namely an "itinerant cinema") had to leave in the morning for the next community on its route.

Most of the movies were from the U.S.A. because French films were not available from occupied Europe. Nevertheless, we were always glad to see the French ones (I remember the funny ones featuring Fernandel, a famous French comedian), even though they were being shown over and over again. The American movies were very entertaining and I became quite partial to the wonderful musicals that were so prevalent in those years. I never tired of the music by George Gershwin (I loved, and still do, the Rhapsody in Blue), and the superb dancing by famous movie superstars as Fred Astaire, Ginger Rogers and Gene Kelly). But, in addition to entertaining us, these movies also helped in another way. Without subtitles, or any dubbing in French, they helped us pick up the English language in a most pleasant and subtle way.

There was something else that helped me to learn

English. It was my interest in American magazines, such as *Life* and *Saturday Evening Post*, that arrived rather regularly through the mail, albeit weeks past their issue dates.I still remember, in particular, the series that ran in the Saturday Evening Post about Tugboat Annie's fast moving adventures. She was the captain of a tugboat and always conquered the challenges that came her way. She could stand her ground against any old salt that was foolish enough to defy her, and she ran her tugboat with an iron fist.

I was an avid reader and enjoyed my books no matter how often I went back to the same ones. And that was a good thing because we had no access to libraries or bookstores, so I had to do with what I brought from Elisabethville. I had books by Jules Verne, Alexander Dumas and Kipling, in addition to a substantial collection of thrillers and adventure stories published by the "Masque" brand of pocket books.

20. More About Life in the Bush

Our move to Lusambo brought about some of the most unsophisticated and unaffected times of our lives. We adapted quite well to an existence without luxuries and modern necessities. Moreover, I should mention also that we might as well have lived in an airtight cocoon because the distress and dread that radiated like wildfire all over the globe at that time, appeared less appalling in our confined environment. After all, we had only limited access to world newscasts and the echoes of war and its cataclysmic developments were obscured by our isolation in the bush.

Here is a little taste of what our life was like in Lusambo.

Living without electricity was not as hard as it sounds. Kerosene portable lanterns took care of general lighting, and our weak short-wave radio ran on batteries. Occasionally, we would catch a broadcast from some distant place, but often we received only static, no matter how many times we tried to extend or reposition the outside antenna. For some unknown reason, reception, such as it was, popped up mostly at night.

The refrigerator ran on kerosene. But it was very temperamental, and it chilled only when the kerosene flame delivered the proper heat level. That flame had to be precisely the right height (set by the adjustable wick), and it had to burn with a particular bluish tint, or we could forget about getting even as little as a trace of coolness from the unreliable contraption. So, when ice supply became available, we switched to an icebox. Delivery consisted of large chunks of ice that were deposited every morning outside our front door, where our house boy, wielding his machete, hacked them into pieces small enough for the icebox. And this brings to mind an incident caused by the ice chips that were left behind by our boy.

Early one morning, before the chips had a chance to melt, the glistening "pebbles" attracted the attention of a couple of hunters walking back to their village. One of them crouched down to examine them, and even picked one up for a better look. But he dropped it at once, because of the unexpected chill that suddenly raced through his fingers, a feeling that he had never experienced before. When he recovered from his consternation, he set a leather pouch on the ground and, with the tip of his spear, pushed several pebbles through the open flap. He made sure not to touch them because it was clear that they possessed strong magical powers and that they were not to be handled with bare fingers. But no risks were going to stop him from bringing the pebbles to the village chief, and receive appropriate rewards for his exceptional courage. The entire village would hail him for his bravery, and he would be admitted to the chief's inner circle. But when he reached the village and rushed to the chief's compound, he discovered that the pebbles had been lifted right out of his pouch, and brazenly replaced by some common water. He knew at once that these were the doings of the other hunter, and immediately went gunning for revenge. This turned into quite a brawl that eventually involved the entire village.

Electricity became available about a year after we came to town. The whole town rejoiced when it first came on, even though power would flow only a few hours each evening. It was quite a luxury. No one thought to complain about the blackouts, no matter how often they occurred. Most of them were the results of storms that knocked tree limbs across the wires, interrupting the transmission of power. As this happened, a few men from the generating plant would go up and down the streets to find the problem and restore power (they used a regular flashlight to see in the dark). Once the trouble was located, they would correct the malfunction with a few jabs of a long bamboo pole and, just like that, our lights would come back up. Admittedly, this may have been a primitive system, but it worked remarkably well under the circumstances.

We drank a lot of water, but not before it was made as safe as possible. This was achieved in three steps; boiling, straining through a filter, and then boiling again for a second time. Mother personally supervised the entire process, and made sure that we always had plenty of good drinking water on hand.

Vegetables were also prepared very carefully. They were never eaten raw, unless they had been washed in a mixture of water and gentian violet. Plus, one had to be cautious with fruits as well. The only safe way to eat them was to wash them before peeling them, so that nothing on the peals would ever contaminate the flesh of the fruits. Father once ate an orange right after he had plucked it from one of our trees and came down with a terrible bout of dysentery. He had to spend three days in the hospital before finally getting well enough to return home. Fortunately, no one else in the family was ever stricken by dysentery, and that was due to mother's fastidious attention to the manner in which raw food was handled in our house. But mother could not protect us from other illnesses. I was stricken with malaria some time after we came to Lusambo, and I remember in particular the throbbing headaches, the chills and the weakness that lasted for weeks. Fortunately, I had caught the mild strain of malaria, and I never faced repeat bouts of the illness. I got malaria when the disease reached epidemic proportions in our area, at the end of a particularly active rainy season. The marshes had enlarged considerably due to the flooding conditions, and that, in turn, helped the mosquito population to explode wildly. But, by the following year the situation had improved dramatically for two reasons. First, fines were collected whenever standing water was found on properties within the town, or its immediate vicinity. That put an end to a multitude of mosquito-breeding puddles. Also, and this was the crucial step, large numbers of Eucalyptus trees were planted about the marshy area because they grew rapidly (remember that the Benguela Railway had planted these fast growing Eucalyptus trees to supply the firewood for their wood burning locomotives), and because they were unusually thirsty. They are nature's topnotch system for draining an area in an efficient and quick way.

We had several mature fruit trees in our yard that supplied us with juicy oranges (they had green peels and were almost as large as grapefruits), tasty tangerines, exquisite mangoes and papayas (I am not using an adjective for the papayas because I never found them to my liking). In addition, the yard had, along one of the perimeter walls, rows of large pineapple plants. There were so many of them that Harry and I used the pineapple fruits for targets when we practiced with the bows and arrows that father bought from a street vendor (after we pestered him to death). We were quite careful when we handled the arrows, as some of the tips could have had some poisonous residue still clinging to the metal (Father did have the gardener clean them thoroughly before allowing us to use them).

Except for some canned goods, our food was produced locally. In our own yard we raised chickens, ducks and rabbits, but even so, most of our "groceries" came from street vendors who peddled all kinds of produce, such as fruits, vegetables, chickens, ducks, goats, eggs and a hodgepodge of artifacts. Our cook helped mother decide what to buy (maybe a goat this time, for the sake of variety), and he also made sure that whatever mother bought was good and fresh. For instance, he immersed eggs in a bucket of water and discarded the ones that floated to the surface. Incidentally, the catholic mission was another source of fresh vegetables. A number of its students would come daily through the white neighborhoods to offer, at very reasonable prices, a profusion of vegetables that had been harvested that very morning in the mission's fields.

The animals that we raised ourselves were well looked after. They lived in a large chicken coop with bamboo walls and a thatch roof, where there was always plenty to eat and drink. But they were not always safe from "common" dangers. One day we heard a large commotion and, when we reached the coop, we saw a boa constrictor in the process of swallowing one of our chickens. We were able to follow the chicken's progress through the reptile, by the way the protruding hump moved along the sides of the long body. The gardener, his machete at the ready, waited until the boa's movements became lethargic (too much food will affect almost anybody the same way) before he cut the head off with a single stroke. Now, this might have been a safe way of dispatching a boa, but not if one wanted to preserve the hide for some good use. If the boa is killed while it swallows its prey, the over-stretched hide becomes paper-thin and practically worthless.

Then there was the time when an army of ants went right through the coop and killed the chickens that could not escape from them. They left mere bones and feathers as calling cards. And that was when father decided that we were going to have an ant-proof coop. He was determined to outfox the voracious ants, and he was going to do so by building the new coop above ground, safely out of the path of their legions. Obviously, that must have been the right approach, because no ants ever harassed our chickens. The new coop was built on sturdy bamboo posts, some four feet off the ground.

That account brings to mind the time that I experimented on one of the chickens that had a strong maternal urge. She would not move aside when the gardener came to collect the daily output of eggs, and tried to defend her nest by striking with her beak. So, what did I do? I swiped her eggs and replaced them with eggs that I took from the ducks' area of the pen. I wanted to see what would happen once they hatched. I did not expect the hen to reject the ducklings offhand, but I did hope for some kind of an interesting development (I did not know precisely what I was looking for, but that did not lessen my perseverance with the experiment). And, to my great amazement, something very interesting did happen. The ducklings hatched in due time and the proud hen took them in a single file around the fenced pen (what a show-off she was). All was well until they reached the area where the resident ducks were swimming in their in-ground tub. Of course, the instant the ducklings saw what was going on, they rushed over and jumped into the water, without giving their mother a chance to do something about it. She rushed after them, but came to a dead stop at the water's edge. And though her motherly instinct was very strong, she could not force herself to jump in. Ultimately, she manifested her distress by flapping her wings, running back and forth and cackling loudly in the direction of her babies. By the time the ducklings finally tired of swimming, the hen was acting like a lunatic and was at the point of losing the last ounce of her sanity. The whole thing was absolutely hilarious, and I decided right then and there that my experiment had been a total success.

There were other experiments, such as the one I tried with the small lizards that often crawled all over our walls and ceilings (their minute suction pads allow them to walk on any surface, even glass). I tried to get close enough to grab them by their tails, and see whether they would escape by leaving their ripped tails writhing in my hands. Unfortunately, I never caught any them, and was not able to prove that they would sacrifice their tails to save their lives.

The most interesting experiment, though, was the one that required me to handle a live scorpion. He had to be alive because I wanted to see whether or not a scorpion in danger of death would commit suicide by plunging the tail's poisonous sting into its own body. My plan was to surround one by a circle of flaming kerosene and see whether he was going to do what was expected of him. But try as I might, I was unable to hold one still enough to pour the kerosene and light a match. They always managed to run away, even when I tried to hold them under an inverted empty tin can. It was frustrating, but the challenges of setting up the experiment were rewards in themselves, as was the fact that I escaped being stung while tempting fate for the sake of knowledge.

There was something interesting about the grass that grew in our yard. It was called "chiendent" (dog's tooth), and it was very tough. The hardy roots crept doggedly in all directions, and gave off new shoots at a rapid growth. As a result, most of the gardener's time was spent mowing the grass by swinging back and forth a narrow strip of metal that was about two inches wide and three feet long. The business end of the metal strip was curved straight out and ground down to fine cutting edges. Those edges were kept appropriately sharp, so that the grass was always trimmed neatly, without any ragged edges. The gardener did such a good job at maintaining the lawn that it looked like part of a golf course.

In addition to the gardener, three other boys worked in our household. First there was the cook, he was the one that moved with us to Leopoldville when father was transferred to the company's headquarters, and actually became an important member of our household. He was trained at Lusambo's Catholic Mission, where he became an excellent chef. His pastries, baguettes, and other crusty breads were first rate, and his meals were unforgettable. I remember the main course called "Moamba", which consisted of chicken cooked in thick red gravy of palm oil infused with pili-pili. He started by boiling the stringy part of the palm nut to extract the unique purplish-red oil. Then he added zest to the oil, by using, among other spices, the fiery pili-pili. This was a red chili pepper that was very hot, and was well liked among the natives who ate it raw - they would put some coarse salt in the palm of their hands, place the pili-pili on top of it, and swallow the combination without so much as a frown. After he was satisfied with the way the oil tasted, he placed the chicken into the boiling concoction and cooked it until well done. This moamba was the favorite meal for entertaining friends on Sunday afternoon, the week's only day of rest (Saturdays were normal working days in those times). Our Christian friends came straight from church and, after the usual aperitif, mother would announce the start of lunch (usually well past 1pm, and Harry and I were often famished by then). The feast would traditionally begin with peanut soup, followed by the moamba, rice and salad, and end with bowls of fresh fruits and some cheeses. There were long intervals between the courses, so that one ate at a leisurely pace, and was able to consume large portions of food with copious amounts of cold beer (kids got lemonade). At any rate, it all added up to a wonderful afternoon, despite the suffocating heat and excessive sweating.

The cook had an assistant who helped with all kinds of chores. He fetched water from the town's spring, looked after the wood supply for the stove, washed dishes, plucked chickens, et cetera.

Finally, there was the house boy. He cleaned the house, served our meals and washed our clothes. He was very good at doing the laundry, from using the sun's rays to bleach our clothes, to ironing them flawlessly with an oversized iron. He kept the iron at the right temperature with a charcoal fire that burned inside the hollow compartment of the appliance. Every once in awhile, he would add more charcoal to it and, after closing the small trap door, he would swing the iron back and forth to create a draft through the side vents, and help the new embers catch fire right away.

Under mother's constant supervision, our house was kept impeccably clean by the house boy. Unfortunately, that did not eliminate the nuisance caused by the ever-present ants and, like everyone else, we learned, to tolerate them as much as was possible. Of course, other insects pestered us

Henri Diamant

as well, but none were as pervasive as those stubborn ants (mosquitoes were in a class by themselves). For instance, we kept our bread, flour, rice, sugar and a variety of condiments in a cupboard that had its four thin legs standing in saucers full of kerosene. And the logic for this was that ants would not dream of wading through kerosene to get at the cupboard's supplies. However, there was another way for them to get in, and they merely dropped from the ceiling, obviously laughing all the way down to the top of the cupboard.

Nothing was ever safe from these ants, or termites for that matter. I still have a couple of books where the termites bore tiny tunnels, from cover to cover, when they invaded our bookcase. The tunnels do not run straight up and down, they wander haphazardly through the pile of pages. When I flip the pages, the tunnels take on a life of their own because they give the impression of moving through the books.

Mother had an unfortunate encounter with a cockroach. It happened one evening while we were relaxing on the veranda with family friends who had come to dinner. The night was unusually dark, but to escape the voracious mosquitoes, we decided against lighting the kerosene lanterns. We could see very little, though we had no difficulty reaching for our drinks and the box of chocolates that our friends had brought with them. But, as we worked our way through the succulent bonbons, mother happened to remark that she especially liked the ones with the raisins. Well, that was when the evening turned on its head. I clearly remember the following succession of events: our guests stated unequivocally that there were no raisins in the bonbons, father rushed to light a lantern, mother looked at what was left of her bonbon, mother saw the partial body of a cockroach, mother gagged and threw up. The evening turned sour.

The following morning, mother laughed off her awful experience, and we went on with our daily activities. Harry and I walked the short distance to school, where assembly was called for eight in the morning. Nuns taught in this whites-only school, which had a grand total of 23 students grouped by grades among the building's three classrooms. First and second grades were in one, third and fourth in another and the fifth and sixth in the last one. Once a student graduated to the seventh grade, he had to go out of town and enroll in a distant boarding school. In Harry's case it was the boarding school in Leopoldville, for the 1941/42 school year, while I followed in his path the succeeding year.

After school, mother usually took us swimming for a couple of hours. The whites-only pool, the size of an Olympic venue, had a row of brick-faced cabanas for changing clothes, and an open-air bowling lane protected by a thatch roof. Several natives, employees of the town, were in charge of the manual system that reset the pins and returned the bowling balls down a rickety wooden ramp. Most Europeans, including missionaries, came to the pool almost daily, but especially on Sundays, when everyone had plenty of leisure time between siestas and the customary dinner parties.

Harry and I spent a lot of time in our yard, keeping

busy with many important projects. We built huts and other contraptions, where we played-out all kinds of thrilling adventures, many of which were clearly detailed in our favorite books, such as the ones about the Swiss Family Robinson, and Robinson Crusoe. Also, we never tired of being around the animals that lived inside the pen. One time we decided to take the rabbits out of their small crates and let them run free with the other animals. And how did they repay us for our kindness? They burrowed under the wire fence and hid all over the yard. Of course, it was back to the crates, once we rounded them up with the grudging help of the gardener.

Our favorite pets were a big part of our lives. We got them through the street peddlers who came daily to our front door, as I mentioned earlier, with all kinds of animals, products, trinkets and handicrafts. Incidentally, some of the artifacts were quite unique. I remember, for instance, the crude toys made of balsa-like wood, the woven baskets that came in various shapes, colors and sizes, the large elephant tusks (some displaying rows of pirogues with fishermen, all finely carved over the entire length of the tusk), and the black adjustable bracelets made from elephant hair. There were also masks, a multitude of carved items, et cetera. But one of the trinkets that I liked quite a bit, was the thumb piano that fitted in the palms of one's hand. These neat miniature pianos were made of progressive-length metal strips that were mounted on a gourd, and were plucked with thumbs to produce cool pleasant sounds.

Oftentimes we bought interesting crafts to decorate our

house, and never tired of haggling with some peddler for an extraordinary object of native handiwork. However, there were items that father would never contemplate acquiring, such as an elephant-leg umbrella stand (gruesome). The legs were cleaved from recent kills, and buried in anthills until the insects consumed all the flesh (they did not gnaw on the hide because of its toughness), and hollowed the legs. Once that process was completed, the legs were left in the sun to dry and turn rigid.

Now, let me go back to our pets.

Our first pet was a black monkey with white facial hair and a very long tail. It had the habit of mimicking native women by wrapping itself in a piece of cloth and parading back and forth on top of the yard wall. The local women got a kick out of that, and always paused to laugh at its antics.

The next pet was a puppy that father bought because we kept pestering him about a dog (we wanted a puppy in the worst way). None of us had a clue about what kind of furry friend he was, and since our boys thought that father knew perfectly well what he had purchased, we were not told at first about his real genealogy. At any rate, he was gorgeous and cuddly, and he took to us the minute the peddler let go of him. And while we noticed that the front legs appeared kind of longer than the ones in the back, and that his ears looked big for the size of his face, we were eager to parade him in front of our friends. So, when several of them came to dinner a couple days later, we did just that. But imagine our dismay when they burst out laughing the minute we entered the living room with our prize. They laughed so hard that they had tears in their eyes. Finally, after regaining composure, they explained that we were holding a hyena, and proceeded to give us some good advice about the breed. But, in the end, none of this mattered because, some weeks later, our puppy died when he fell off the veranda while chasing after a lizard. We had become very attached to the little guy, and the loss hit us very hard.

My favorite of all pets was a green parrot named Coco. He was quite young when he came to us via the usual peddler's way and, since he was not a grey parrot (grey African parrots are pricey because of their uncanny ability to talk), we got him for a pittance. He had a perch on the veranda, but never hesitated to make himself at home all over the apartment. One of his favorite places was the veranda handrail facing the direction of our school. He perched there while he waited for us to return from school, and screached his head off when we appeared around the corner of the street. Mother always knew when we were about to get home. Moreover, he ended up talking perfectly well, because no one ever told him that he was not supposed to do so. It started one day as we were having our meal, and the cook showed up to ask what mother wanted from him. Actually, mother had not called, and he left the dining room, mumbling all the way back to the kitchen. But a few minutes later he came again, and that was when mother became irritated - he shows up when not needed, and does not come when called for- she observed aloud. However, as the cook came in for a third time, we were suddenly surprised to hear mother's voice calling him from some place outside the room. And that was how we found, to our great delight, that Coco had orchestrated this entire confusion and could talk as well as his grey cousins. Afterward, I also noticed that, without any doubt whatsoever, he actually knew what he was saying. For instance, there was the episode of the peanuts, his favorite food. As was typical, he ate on his perch, standing on one foot while using the other to grip tightly the peanut pod that he had taken from his feeding cup. Ordinarily, he would crack the pod with his beak, choose one of the peanuts and drop everything else to the ground (what can I say? He was a very messy eater). Well, this particular time, both peanuts dropped out of the pod before he had a chance to grab one for himself. He turned his head horizontally so that one eye could see straight down, looked at those elusive peanuts laying in the mess around his perch and let go, with perfect timing, the fitting French expletive word of "merde". Well, now you understand that I was not merely bragging about Coco when I said that he knew what he was saying. This event was the irrefutable proof of his great intelligence. At any rate, he was truly the perfect pet, and his personality was so entrancing that we never again tormented our parents about a replacement for our dearly departed "puppy".

While all this was going on, father was busy managing the store, and doing his best to keep sales going in the face of ever diminishing supplies. Fortunately, he became very innovative at finding good substitutes for almost anything, and was thus able to maintain business at a decent clip. For instance, when tanned leather became unavailable for the replacement of worn soles, father used raw hides.

He purchased these raw hides from the natives, and had them stretched over sturdy frames that were set up in an open area of our back yard. There, they were left to cure and dry, by the relentless rays of the sun. And voila, in no time at all, father had enough soling material on hand to keep the repair workshop open for business. Of course, the end-result was hairy on one side and rock-hard all over, but the material had a decent abrasive quality and was deemed fully satisfactory under the circumstances (one had to learn to live with the shortages caused by war). Obviously, anything was better than walking with holes in the bottom of your shoes. And when supplies of new footwear dried up, father was able to lay hands on bales of used dresses that helped immeasurably in maintaining a decent cash flow in the business (that father resorted to the same strategy in Elisabethville). For safety reasons, European ladies were given first choice whenever new bales came in, and only after they had made their purchases, was the general public allowed in the store. This frequently resulted in a buying frenzy, and required the presence of a couple of policemen to maintain peace among the native customers.

Father also achieved a considerable amount of publicity and goodwill by performing pedicure procedures whenever a particular need arose among our fellow expatriates. His pedicure implements were always at the ready (it was the same set that he had used in Czechoslovakia) and everything he did was invariably free of charge. Father treated ingrown nails, painful corns and anything else that had to do with feet, including poor circulation. His massages became famous because they always helped people, and inevitably made them feel better.

Among father's many extraordinary achievements and successes, the most momentous was the Sales Course for Retail Personnel, which he created within months of taking over the Lusambo store. It is a tribute to his foresight and managerial acumen, to have determined early on that Africans had to be trained for future positions of responsibility - and at a time when it was judged a sacrilege to even think of natives in those terms. At any rate, father promoted this idea throughout his entire career and, a couple of years before retiring, he organized a permanent training school, with teaching staff and a full curriculum, within the headquarters of N'Dolo, Leopoldville. The trainees became known as the "Diamant Boys" and, as time went on, most attained good positions in the company. Thus, when father eventually retired, the 1959 February/March N'Dolo Digest (Bata's bi-monthly bulletin) carried the following article - "Upon arrival in our country, Monsieur Diamant adapted quickly to the Congolese mentality and with great success managed our retail division in the district of Kasai. Yet, he did not concentrate merely on sales and profits, he also fought hard to set up locally, for the first time in the existence of our entire organization, a training program for future salesmen and managers. Some of these early trainees became exceptionally successful in our company, such as Monsieur Bernard Tshibambe, manager in Usumbura, and Monsieur Andre Lubaki, supervisor for African Sales in Leopoldville".

21. The Eventful Year of 1942

The year of 1942 turned out to be quite remarkable.

It became notable mainly for two reasons. First, because I went off to boarding school, and second, but not least, because our sister Eliska (Czech version of Elise -endearing version actually) decided to make her grand entrance on the world scene soon after I left Lusambo. Furthermore, this was the year that the family moved to Leopoldville.

Harry had left to attend boarding school for the 1941/1942 scholastic year. For the first time ever, I had to manage without his company. Initially, that was pretty hard, but my pets helped greatly and I also kept busy with different local happenings. For instance, I spent most of a day one time observing the natives hunt by bush-fire, on the opposite bank of the Sankuru River. They lit a line of fire that formed a broken circle, and patiently waited around the narrow opening, with spears and arrows at the ready. As the flames moved relentlessly toward the center of the circle, terrified prey tried to flee through the break, right into the path of the hunters. Only a few lucky ones escaped the ambush. The flames eventually met in the center and formed a whirlwind that extinguished the fire abruptly. Then, as the ground cooled well enough for bare feet, women with baskets on their backs moved through the area to gather snakes, rats, birds and anything else that the fire left behind. Nothing was wasted and every hunter received a fair portion of the bush-meat. The choicest portions were saved for the village chief, the master of the bush.

Another time I accompanied Dr. Reznik, one of the two doctors in the hospital, and a good friend of the family (he was the one who delivered Eliska), on an inspection tour of several outlying clinics. Much to my dismay, I could not stop throwing up, and was miserable all day long. I had not been in a vehicle ever since we arrived from Elisabethville, and obviously that brought about the awful case of carsickness. This was the first and last time that I stepped into a car while in Lusambo. Anyway, the only other thing that sticks in my mind about this fateful trip, is that we almost ran into a huge tree when we skidded on large piles of dung left behind by a herd of elephants.

At any rate, time flew by rather quickly, and suddenly Harry was home for summer recess. In the Congo, summer recess lasted only a few weeks since the school year was divided into trimesters, and considerable vacation periods were given between academic periods.

On one hand I wanted to see these two months go on forever, but I also longed impatiently for the end of the vacation, because that was when Harry and I were scheduled to take off together for the boarding school in Leopoldville, a brand new experience for me (first time away from home, first time traveling by plane). As Harry had done before me, I had finally graduated from the top grade of our tiny school and had to move to a larger educational institution. And though Harry warned me that life in a boarding school was full of hardships, I could not contain my excitement about the new direction that my destiny was taking.

Eventually, the time came for the two of us to wave a final goodbye to our parents and climb into a big Sabena DC3 (the Fokker Wulfes were being replaced at the time by the newer and faster DC3s). The inside cabin had room for more than 20 passengers and looked absolutely cavernous to me. The flight was full - there were no unoccupied seats on board. As we strapped ourselves in, Harry pointed to small bags piled neatly between the seats and the bulkhead, and explained that they contained industrial diamonds on the way to the war effort in the USA.

The door was closed and the airplane taxied at a leisurely pace through the grass, toward the hill at the end of the runway. Once properly lined up, the brakes were locked hard, both engines were brought to full power and the pilot ran through a final check of all the instruments. Then, the brakes were released and the aircraft leapt forward.

We were hardly airborne when the airplane made a low-level turn over the Sankuru River and headed toward our stop over in Luluabourg. But do not think for one second that I enjoyed my new experience. A few minutes into the flight I became nauseated and had to use the airsickness paper bags all the way to Luluabourg. What a drag that was. The end of the flight could not have come early enough for me.

When we landed, a Sabena agent stepped into the cabin and asked for two volunteers that were inclined to give up their seats, and wait a couple of days in Luluabourg, for the next schedule flight to Leopoldville. The two seats were needed to make room for a stretcher with a gravely ill person waiting to be airlifted to the capital's hospital.

Well, as far as Harry and I were concerned, this was the ultimate break, the finest opportunity that we could have ever hoped for. Harry wanted to delay, as much as possible, another confinement in the boarding school. I wanted desperately to delay, for as long as possible, another confrontation with airsickness.

Sabena put us up at the town's finest hotel and made us feel like real VIPs. But little did we know that our decision to give up our seats, was to result in an unexpected consequence. It brought about the premature birth of Eliska.

We were to be met at Leopoldville's airport by Monsieur Kon, who worked in the company's office, and who had promised our parents to deliver us to the boarding school. Since we failed to appear, he telegraphed father to ask about our delay, and to get our new flight information. Well, this telegram scared mother out of her wits, and she promptly went into labor. She was rushed to the hospital, where Eliska was born several days prematurely. But, though Eliska's timing was off, her birth occurred appropriately in a most outstanding spot for a brand new and "precious" Diamant... an area rich in the other kind of diamonds.

And this brings to mind another true story, where our family's name became embroiled briefly with those rich deposits of diamonds, and almost wrecked a friend's trip to the USA.

It all started innocuously enough, when father asked a friend who was about to leave for New York, to meet with our Aunt Johanna, and to give her the latest news about us. Well, his long trip proceeded well enough until he reached New York's Idlewild Airport (Kennedy Airport) and tried to go through customs. To his surprise, he was isolated from the other passengers and grilled for hours on end about his occupation and life in Lusambo. Finally, when it was almost one in the morning and he was on the point of breaking down from exhaustion, one of the agents asked about an entry in his notebook. Specifically, the one about "Pas oublier les Diamants" (do not forget the diamonds). And since he had come from the Kasai region, this particular message was obviously suspicious, and would he please tell them where he had hidden the gems.

But all is well that ends well. He explained what the note was all about; the customs agent called our aunt to verify her maiden name and, at long last, allowed our unfortunate friend leave the terminal.

22. History of Leopoldville

As our flight proceeded ever closer to Leopoldville, the forested region underneath the wings gave way to a savanna landscape crisscrossed by rivers flowing toward the mighty Congo River. Then came some hills and, a little farther on, the huge Stanley Pool, the lake created by the Congo River. The plane dropped down over the water, lined up with the runway and, after barely clearing a fishing village on stilts, touched down on N'Dolo Airport's single runway. We had finally arrived in Leopoldville.

Sir Henry Stanley had set up a trading post on this location in 1881, and named it Leopoldville in honor of King Leopold ll, the absolute ruler of the Congo Free State. Immediately downstream are the Livingstone Rapids, a succession of roaring cataracts that plunge the river some 900 feet in the relatively short distance of 220 miles, and choke off all navigation between Leopoldville and the ocean. The city is built on the south bank of the lake, opposite the city of Brazzaville, capital of the Republic of the Congo. Initially, the Republic of the Congo was part of a federation of French colonial possessions in North-central Africa, known as French Equatorial Africa, which extended northward from the Congo River. The cities are only a couple of miles apart across the water, making this the only place on earth where two capitals lie within eyesight of each other.By the way, this proximity became extremely advantageous when, in the early days of the war, it became imperative to replace Brazzaville's Vichy-leaning administration by one that supported General Charles DeGaulle and his Free French Forces. The importance of this switch cannot be overstated because it kept Germany from gaining control of the French colonies and their important resources of raw materials. It is really scary to think what might have happened if the German war machinery would have won easy access to the uranium, industrial diamonds, copper, et cetera, that are so abundant on the African continent.

At any rate, it was a small contingent of French and British officers, supported by some Congolese troops, that crossed over to Brazzaville and, in the middle of a very dark night, captured the French Governor General without bloodshed. He was dragged to Leopoldville, where he was thrust into an airplane and flown to England. Subsequently, General DeGaule designated Brazzaville as the capital of the Free French Forces and appointed Felix Eboue as the Governor General of French Equatorial Africa (all this happened in 1940). Governor Felix Eboue, the first African official to have reached the highest level of the French administration, proved to be an unwavering supporter of the General, and a man wholly committed to the struggle for a free France. He remained in office until his death in 1944. The country honored him by entombing him in Paris' Pantheon, right alongside other famous Frenchmen, such as

Voltaire, Rousseau, and Hugo.

General DeGaulle traveled often to Brazzaville and, on occasion, took the ferry across the lake to pay an official visit to Leopoldville. I was at the river's landing during one of these visits, and saw him up close. To this day I marvel at the height of the man. He was 6' 5" tall.

Here are additional notes about the Congo River, the city of Leopoldville and other relevant subjects.

Since there was no way to navigate over the rapids, a railway was built around them in 1898. That closed the transportation gap and transformed Leopoldville into the leading transit point between the Atlantic and the western regions of the colony. In 1920, Leopoldville became the capital of the Congo, taking the title away from the less developed town of Boma, on Congo's estuary.

The single-track railroad starts at the river-port of Matadi, some 93 miles from the Atlantic coast. Ocean going vessels can not proceed upriver any farther than that, due to the forbidding cataracts that rule upstream from Matadi. Even between the Atlantic and Matadi, sailing is full of hazards, such as the infamous whirlpool that forms the Devil's Cauldron, the straying sandbars and the challenging right-angle turns in the river's course.

By the end of the war, however, the railroad became unable to cope with the ever-increasing volume of imports, and incoming goods were trapped for many weeks on the docks. The transit time to Leopoldville took longer than most ocean crossings from overseas ports. Really quite an ironic situation considering that cargo from New York needed only two weeks to get to Matadi, but more than two months to cover the 220 miles between Matadi and Leopoldville. This problem was also compounded by the fact that the dirt road connecting the two cities was often impassable, especially for heavy trucks.

The European area of Leopoldville was clean and bustling, with affluent residential and commercial neighborhoods. The major avenue was the Boulevard Albert Ier. It started at King Albert's monument in front of the Railroad Station and extended all the way to the opposite side of town. It was wide, flanked by trees and the median strip was full of flowering bushes. As a matter of fact, Leopoldville was known as the Garden City because trees, bushes and flowers grew all over the metropolitan area.

The town had a multitude of retail stores, and even a cinema where movies were shown twice a week, on Saturdays and Wednesdays. Utilities, such as electricity, telephone and running water were supplied all over the metropolitan area.

Most of the year, the weather was hot and stuffy, and the abundant rains kept the humidity extremely high. Since this was before air conditioning became easily available, the only way to cool off was to spend time at the city's pool, the Funa Club. In addition to a large pool, the Funa offered several tennis courts with ball boys.

The dominant native language was Liguala. It was a Bantu language that became, after independence, the lingua franca of the population, while French remained the official language of the linguistically diverse country.

The Governor General ruled the colony from a large government complex in town, and his directives were put into effect by the five Provincial Governors who controlled their individual provinces. It was Belgium's efficient way of reigning over its colony without worrying about local representation.

23. Boarding School

Madame and Monsieur Kon met us at the airport, and told us about our brand new sister Eliska. A sister! Well, at first I did not know what to make of it because, in my frame of mind, a brother would have been more appropriate. But then, the notion grew on me and I started looking forward to the time when I would see her for the very first time.

We collected our suitcases and were taken straight from the airport to our boarding school, the College Albert Ier, where the faculty members happened to be Jesuit Priests - the strictest disciplinarians and the most demanding teachers in the entire Catholic priesthood (how lucky can one get). The discipline was so rigorous that, even after many years had passed, this tough experience helped me sail easily through the basic training at the United States Naval Training Center in Bainbridge, Maryland.

The campus had several modern structures on the periphery of a big playing field for soccer games and other athletic activities. In addition to the faculty's quarters, the buildings held large and airy classrooms, a chapel and a great auditorium, but no actual dormitories or even a dining hall. We slept in converted classrooms, and ate across the street, in a dining hall located within the College Sacre Coeur, a school for girls run by Nuns. Some years later, Eliska attended this school as a day student.

From day one, I became exposed to the most structured way of life. Reveille came by way of imperious whistle-blows that woke us abruptly from deep sleep. We had to leap from our beds, line up in the aisles and stand at attention. All this without uttering a single word. Then, other whistle-blows, and we walked to the showers - whistle, and we used the showers - whistle, and we walked out of the showers - whistle, well you get the idea.

Once we were properly dressed and our beds were made up, we formed into lines for our walk across the street, and breakfast. At that point, we were finally allowed to talk, but only if the instructor was fully satisfied with our conduct (permission was given by that arrogant whistle). After breakfast, the daily mass (no excuses given to Harry and me - we had to be there, but we were not expected to participate in the prayers), some free time and, at 8 o'clock, the start of classes.

Classes went on until noon and, after siesta, resumed at 2 o'clock. School disbanded at 4 o'clock, and the day students went home, while we began to study and play games until 6 o'clock.

After dinner, free time and vespers (a short evening service in the chapel), we landed in bed around 8 o'clock.

Once in a while, we were treated to movies in the auditorium. And once a month, we were allowed to spend a day with Madame and Monsieur Kon because our parents had authorized them to take us off the school property. We would go to a soccer match and end the day with a delicious home-cooked meal.

Discipline was enforced with a heavy hand, and no disorderly conduct was ever tolerated. Usual punishment consisted of day-old bread and a glass of water, as a substitute for lunch, and a ton of written exercises intended to last through the siesta recess.

On Sundays, when we were not with the Kons, we were kept busy with athletic activities, study periods and leisure times. Harry often used part of his leisure time keeping an eye out for Pan Am's weekly flying boat that flew over our heads on Sunday afternoons. It took off from the Stanley Pool, flew laboriously across the school grounds and then turned south, toward Cape Town, South Africa, at the very bottom of the African continent. The roar of its engines was deafening, and its size boggled the mind, no matter how often one saw it. Personally, I was not very interested by all this because, unlike Harry, I had not yet acquired a passion for aviation. However, that changed drastically later on in my life.

I was good at staying out of trouble and, for much of the time, had no real problems with the harsh discipline. Nevertheless, I was thrilled the day Monsieur Kon told us that our parents were moving to Leopoldville and that, before long, we would be living at home... and with our new sister.

24. New Bata Factory

As the war in Europe progressed, supplying the retail chain got more and more difficult, until it became evident that the only alternative to closing down was to start producing some of the footwear in the colony. And so, it was decided to set up a factory, in one way or another, within Leopoldville's urban area, where reliable electric power was readily available.

Father's intensive experience in the shoe-repair process, which incidentally operates with some of the same systems and machinery that are often found in footwear manufacturing operations, made him the perfect fit for the task at hand. As a result, he was transferred to Leopoldville, and asked to work on a game plan for a rapid jump-start of production.

There were several prerequisites that had to be put in place. The first, obviously, was some kind of structure large enough to support the manufacturing process. Then there was the need for machinery, manufacturing supplies, trained workers, et cetera.

It would have been a daunting undertaking under the best of circumstances, but not for the determined team of a half dozen, or so, dedicated and loyal company men who were gathered in Leopoldville at that crucial time.

In any event, even with very limited funds, and a mess of overwhelming obstacles, they accomplished their goal with superb results.

This is how it all came together.

As luck would have it, they were able to hunt down an unused barge-repair facility in an industrial suburb of town, right on the bank of the Stanley Pool. It was a large walled compound with several villas for Europeans and a number of hangars suitable for all kinds of manufacturing processes. It had access to electricity and running water, and extended from the lakeside to the road that connected the town to the N'Dolo Airport. The team, recognizing immediately the great potential of this property, managed to lease it for a song, and even obtained a ten-year option-to-buy contract, at a knocked down price. And this turned out to be the deal of the century because, as the town began to expand toward the airport area, the value of the property increased a hundred-fold within a few years.

It did not take long to clear the stubborn vegetation that had overrun most of the compound, make the villas livable for the team, and set up an office in one of the hangars. However, the tough part was to get rid of the reptiles that had infested the place. Initially, all gardeners and workers were given financial incentives for dead snakes that they brought in for inspection and tally. Once counted and paid for, the reptiles were buried at the foot of an enormous baobab tree, in the back area of the compound. Nevertheless that system of incentives had to be called off when it became evident that the natives were taking advantage of the circumstances. Instead of wasting time hunting dangerous snakes, they dug out the dead reptiles and pocketed their rewards a second time around. After all, the white man was fair game, and craftiness a de facto policy of the country. The natives must have planned their clever subterfuge from day one. Why else would they bury the reptiles, instead of dumping them effortlessly into the lake?

The next step was the start-up of a rudimentary tannery that utilized the vegetable-tanning process, since this method does not require a complicated set-up. All that had to be done was to dig pits, make them completely waterproof and fill them with water containing a tannin extracted from the bark of trees, like the mimosa tree (hence the designation of "vegetable-tanning process"). The actual tanning process was easy - first the hides were soaked in a lime solution, then the hair and flesh were scraped off with a large dull knife, and finally they were immersed in the pits. Several weeks later, they came out of the pits as fully tanned leather (this is an abridged description of the process). It was a neat process, albeit with one a drawback. The awful smell given off by the tannery was extremely overpowering at times.

Several parts of the project were beginning to fit together like pieces of a puzzle. There was the tannery that was about to produce leather, workshops that were ready to accept machinery, and a handful of workers who were being trained for various jobs. Father taught them how to cut patterns out of hides (an experienced cutter produces the maximum possible number of components from each skin, and minimizes the amount of unusable remnants), the correct way to stitch leather with awl and thread, et cetera.

However, two important elements were still missing - machinery and related equipment. But, here again, luck was on the side of the project. The team heard about some shoe-making machinery and equipment stockpiled in northern Angola, and a couple of them left immediately to inspect the equipment first hand. They drove for many exhausting days over very primitive and dangerous roads, but the outcome was worth the hardships because the equipment turned out to be a real bonanza. A deal was struck and, several months later, the equipment showed up at the factory.

In the meantime, the tannery delivered its first lot of finished leather, which was turned over to a workshop that father had set up to produce a limited line of hand made suitcases. These suitcases were indestructible because they were made of thick bottom-leather, the kind normally used for resoling shoes. And though they were extremely heavy, they sold like hot cakes. Weight was not an issue when there was nothing else on the market.

Father also found an excellent way to utilize the scraps of leather that were left over from the production of the suitcases. He turned waste into consumer products, mostly doormats. Scraps were cut into symmetrical pieces, and then holes were punched in their centers so that they could be threaded over steel wires in a multitude of alternating patterns.

The N'Dolo Digest of March 1959 which featured an article about father's retirement, also said something about his role in the factory's start up.

"The destiny of our production was entrusted to Monsieur Diamant when he transferred to Leopoldville. He lived through the most difficult period of our company. But his competence, keen sense of improvisation and high popularity among the workers, helped to thrust our factory's early production onto a fast track and created a nucleus of trained personnel that became the key to the rapid expansion of our manufacturing capacity".

Money was in short supply during those days. And while workers and suppliers were always paid in full, the team members did with what little was left over at the end of each month. I can still remember father breaking cigarettes in two because that made them last longer.

In the end, hard work and perseverance overcame all obstacles and, by the time war ended, the company owned a fully operational factory in the Congo, a factory that had not been planned or financed by Headquarters. It was a thriving factory set on a very valuable piece of real estate.

25. Bimbo the Chimp

Except for Madame and Monsieur Kon, and our family, the other expatriates were single men that Zlin had assigned to various African posts before the start of the war. Most of the men, had sweethearts back home and planned to marry them at the end of the hostilities. However, two of them were able to make their marital moves ahead of the others when they volunteered in the Czech Army in England and fought their way to their respective home-towns with the first wave of liberating allied troops. Within weeks, one married his sweetheart, while the other wedded the younger sister of his former darling. That flame had fallen in love with another man and had married during the war. Both couples left Europe as soon as post-war travel restrictions eased off, and came straight to Leopoldville where the men resumed their careers with the company.

We lived next to the Kons, on one side of the compound, while the single expatriates paired up in the remaining villas- these were large stucco homes with corrugated metal roofs and a profusion of big windows. Past neglect was obvious on the rundown exteriors, but the restored interiors, with their large rooms, high ceilings, and cross-ventilation, were rather pleasant.

Our tiny community also included a two-story building

that held some offices on the first floor, and a social club on the second floor where all the single men had their meals. It was run as a cooperative organization and each man took turns to manage the club for one month at a time, being personally responsible for everything connected with it, such as daily expenses, personnel, menus, et cetera. When we first moved to the compound, I spent hours lounging at one of the club's second floor windows to watch for trains that used the track on the opposite side of the road. I had not seen trains since we had moved from Elisabethville and it took a while before I lost interest in railroads. Incidentally, that track was the lone track that connected Leopoldville to Matadi and helped open the interior of the country to the outside world. Little did I know that one day I would be a passenger on the train called "Train Blanc" (White Train) rolling over this same track on the first leg of my journey to the U.S.A., via Matadi and Boma.

Congenial, full of fun and enlivened by a variety of pets-dogs, monkeys, leopards, and a chimp named Bimbo, life in the compound was ready made for Harry and me. These animals were not owned, in a strict sense, by any individual in particular, despite who may have purchased them. The animals were a marvelous aspect of life at the compound. The one exception was the leopard that, in the end, turned out to be too difficult to handle by anyone. He was donated to the local zoo, hardly a couple of months after he came into our lives.

Bimbo, the chimp, was quite a character. To start with, she always managed to escape from her cage, no matter how sturdy it was at the time, or how well the door was padlocked. As a result, she roamed freely all over the compound and whenever she got bored and wanted to attract attention, she turned outright mischievous. For instance, she would disturb the calm of the day's siesta by raising as much racket as possible. She would crouch on her haunches on a villa's front step, with her back against the door and a tin can firmly clutched in her hand. Thus positioned, she would create a resounding noise by dragging the tin can along the rough surface of the step, and, rocking back and forth, produce a loud pounding noise by striking the front door with the full might of her muscular back. She certainly earned attention by doing this, but not the kind she longed for.

Craving people's food was another nasty habit of hers. She would creep into one of the homes (breaking into homes was apparently as easy as overcoming the padlocks of her cage), go straight to the kitchen and help herself to the tastiest tidbits in the refrigerator. But that was not all she did; deliberately, she would sink her teeth into more food than she could abscond with. She knew darn well that this would make it unpalatable to humans, and that she would end up getting the whole lot in the long run.

Bimbo loved to disrupt our tennis games when Harry and I played against each other or when we honed our shots at the practice wall. She would sneak onto the court, grab several tennis balls and run away before the boys could stop her. She took great pleasure in messing up our games because she knew instinctively that she had the upper hand

and would not be taken to task by us. Wisely she did not dare to bother adults and never misbehaved when they used the court. This was a first class red-clay tennis court that was built in the back of the compound, within yards of the lake and the big baobab tree of the reptile-incident fame. However, because of this proximity to the water, at times crocodiles crawled up to the court to warm themselves on the sun-heated clay and enjoy a pleasant relief from the cold surroundings of the river's depths. The boys usually chased them away when they had to start preparing the court for the day's games.

In the end, it was not her prankish disposition that landed Bimbo in the local zoo. What did her in, was one of the mightiest of all instincts- called motherhood. Unfortunately, no one recognized what was happening, even after she started to display an unusual affinity for Eliska, and would come running whenever our sister was taken out for a stroll in her baby carriage. As a matter of fact, I have recently found a photograph where father is lifting Bimbo by her elbows so she could peek in the baby carriage and gaze at Eliska. Maybe no one noticed this budding problem because Bimbo never attempted to touch or harm our sister in any way whatsoever. But, one dreadful day, when a lady and her baby came to visit us, much to everyone's consternation, Bimbo snatched the baby right out of its carriage, and lovingly carried it up to the top of the nearest tree. Then, for what seemed like an eternity, she kept on refusing to bring it back down (no one dared to climb after her, for fear that she would drop the baby). When, after a lot of cajoling, she finally came down and swapped the baby for a bunch of plump bananas, she was promptly and altogether unceremoniously jostled into a crate and carted off immediately to the zoo. We did not even have the time to say a proper goodbye to her. However, we frequently went to see her at the zoo and she always seemed happy to see us.

Harry and I spent long hours playing with pirogues and sailing to nearby islands. We had no trouble getting our hands on those pirogues because large storms usually swept them down from some upriver riverbanks, and they were easily grabbed as they floated among clumps of water hyacinth and chunks of plant matter. At times, especially when we got our hands on a particularly large pirogue, we erected a mast and, thanks to some old sheets surrendered by mother, sailed leisurely around our watery playground. Anyway, there was no danger of being swept away because we were quite a distance from the rapids, and the current was manageable in our particular expanse of the Stanley Pool.

Camping was another activity that we always enjoyed, especially when it included most of the residents of our compound. We would pile up into cars and head for a small sandy beach on the bank of the river, right where it narrows down and begins to form some of the first rapids. Other times we would decide to camp in the forest, where a clear streamlet flowed down to the river. Mother and Lily would set up the food (bottles were immersed in the running water to keep the drinks cool), while the men kept the camp-fire going, practiced with their rifles, played cards or merely relaxed on some thick blankets.

Fred was an avid hunter and never missed an opportunity to go after all kinds of game. One day, while we camped on the riverbank, he killed an immense crocodile that must have devoured a human because body parts were found in his gut. On the other hand, father was only an occasional hunter, and when he finally decided to take me along, I must have been around14 years old. We drove deep into the savanna and, in no time at all, came upon a pack of antelopes grazing in the distance. Father fired his rifle and one of them dropped to the ground, while the rest took off in a mad free-for-all. The one that father hit was still breathing when I reached it, and in my mind I can still see those big brown eyes staring back at me with one of the saddest looks that I had ever seen before or since.

That was the first and last hunt of my life.

As team sports go, soccer was very popular, and we often enjoyed attending fiercely competitive matches in the town's stadium. In fact, the company supported its own soccer team, which eventually became very famous and, as a result, helped promote the Bata brand among the local population. There were, though, embarrassing moments during some of their matches. Without fail, whenever they started to fall behind and were in danger of losing the game, the players would kick off their customized Bata soccer boots and, more often than not, go on winning the match in their bare feet. Dumping shoes is not what one would call an appropriate action for a team representing a footwear company.

A final thought comes to mind about those times. It is

about the vacation that we spent in Pointe Noire, an Atlantic port on the coast of French Equatorial Africa. Mother, Eliska, Harry and I hopped on the Brazzaville ferry and then boarded a plane that went straight to the coast. Pointe Noire was only a small village in those days, with an active port, an airbase and miles upon miles of pristine white beaches. The town's only hotel was a short walking distance from the shore, and the clear lukewarm waters of the ocean. The only fly-in-the-ointment was the over-heated sand that burned our feet whenever we left the cool shade under our private clump of palm trees.

26. D-Day and the Move to Elizabethville

Time flew by, and all of a sudden, we found ourselves in the momentous year of 1944.

On the sixth of June, the day that became known as D-Day, Allied troops stormed the Normandy beaches, and within five days overran eighty miles of the French coast. The war in Europe was being won. The carnage was about to cease in that part of the world. Father immediately contacted the Red Cross and asked whether they could provide some information about the fate of our family. Months later, the report that we received turned out to be even more dreadful than the dark desperation that had filled our worst nightmares. As I stated earlier, our immediate family was all but annihilated.

Meanwhile, as the factory's production continued to exceed everyone's hopes, it became necessary to expand the retail chain and set up a network of independent distributors. So, in due time father returned to the Retail Division and took over the district of Katanga, where a substantial economic boom was expected upon cessation of hostilities (the expansion of Katanga's mining industry was to figure greatly in the efforts to rebuild Europe).

Once more, we packed our possessions and said goodbye to friends and pets. We flew all the way across the country, back to Elisabethville, a town that had grown robustly since we left it so many years ago.

We moved into a nice villa, in a brand new development on the edge of town, and Harry and I rejoined the student body of good old College Saint Francois de Sales.

Our new neighborhood lacked paved roads, and there was no escaping the red dust that covered everything in sight. However, Katanga's more moderate temperatures made up for any inconvenience, and we thoroughly enjoyed the change from the brutal weather that was so prevalent in Leopoldville. As a matter of fact, expatriates, living in other parts of the Congo, who were recovering from some particularly debilitating disease, came often to Elisabethville to recuperate in its healthier climate. And that was exactly why our parents invited an associate from Leopoldville, who had been very ill, to come to Elisabethville to regain his health as a guest in our house.

In itself, this visit was not exceptionally noteworthy. However, it happily concluded in a most extraordinary way, as far as Harry and I were concerned, because the grateful guest presented us with a motorbike. He really meant to give us a couple of bicycles, but since supply had not yet caught up with demand, and none were available at the time, he decided to go for the only thing that he unearthed. It was a beautiful, although slightly battered, red motorbike. It was small, really only a couple of steps above a moped, and its top speed was unimpressive (if I remember correctly, it had a single cylinder motor, rated at 175cc, that ran on a mixture of gas and oil). Our guest figured that we could not get hurt riding this lightweight version of a motorcycle.

And yes, initially our parents were opposed to the gift, but we finally convinced them to let us keep it by promising to ride only over the back roads of the bush, and never, but never, use it in town. What a sweet victory that was.

We enjoyed many terrific hours on that motorbike, especially after we discovered a beautiful area, within an hour's ride from the house, where a brook flowed out of a small lake and went on its way through some widespread grasslands. It was ready-made for camping, fishing, and all kinds of interesting activities.

Once in a while, the motorbike would act temperamentally and refuse to start. When that happened for the first time, we tried to revive it by pushing the stubborn machine down a hill and releasing the clutch once it moved at a fast clip. It did not work; the engine chose to remain brutally obstinate and summarily refused to exhibit any signs of life, no matter how often we tried the maneuver. So, as we were at the point of asking father for help, we decided to make use of our tool kit and attempt to find out what was bothering the engine. We took it apart (that was not complicated because there were few parts to contend with) and eventually identified the problem ourselves. The red dust had found its way into the mechanism and was choking the engine to death. We cleaned everything in some turpentine and, after replacing all the parts in their proper places, were able to start the engine at the first try. Its strong and steady purring made our hearts jump with joy.

This was a good time for us, except for the fact that no

pets were part of the family. We did get a puppy when we first arrived, but unfortunately it perished when a car ran over it. Everyone was terribly sad at the loss, and mother decided, then and there, that no more pets would break our hearts in the future... It took almost five years before our next pet came into our lives.

The end of the European war had its beginnings during the invasion on D-Day, June of 1944. Paris was liberated that August and Belgium became free in September.

Then 1945 rolled around, and with it Peace throughout the World. German emissaries came to General Eisenhower's headquarters in Reims, France, and signed an unconditional surrender. This document was ratified in Berlin on May 8, 1945.

General Douglas MacArthur accepted Japan's unconditional surrender when the Emperor's representatives boarded the battleship SS Missouri, anchored in the middle of Tokyo Bay, and signed the proper documents on September 2, 1945.

The war was finally over.

Unfortunately, the end of the war did not clinch the kind of peace that mankind was hoping for. It did not abolish discrimination, carnage or cruelty. It brought about the end of colonialism and, notably, the break up of the British Empire, an Empire where the sun never set. Unfortunately, much blood was spilled in the process, which also released pent up hostilities between religious factions (such as between the Hindus and the Muslims in India/Pakistan) and, even right now, aggression still erupts periodically between adherents of opposing religions.

Thus far, one heartening exception to this sad fact is the peace that evolved between the Catholic and Protestant factions of Northern Ireland. No one thought it would ever come, yet it happened despite the vicious killings that both sides perpetrated over many years.

The end of the war also set off the forces that partitioned the world into two main camps, Capitalism and Communism, freedom and repression. This went on for several decades, but the communist culture finally lost out to freedom. Of course, the outcome was never in doubt. I still remember what many Czechs had to say about the Soviet experience; "We may be able to endure another Nazi occupation, but never again another Soviet liberation".

27. Tonsillitis and Cape Town

I remember clearly that I was feeling under the weather during the early part of 1945. It started with an occasional pain in my throat and some bouts of fever. Before long, this progressed to headaches, nausea and some difficulties in swallowing.

It took a few weeks, but eventually I was diagnosed with the worst case of tonsillitis that the doctor had ever seen. Germs from the infected tonsils had invaded other parts of my body, and my health was deteriorating rapidly. The tonsils had to be removed as quickly as possible.

I was taken to the hospital, where the surgeon proceeded to remove my tonsils. And I should mention, by the way, that this particular surgeon had quite a reputation in town. Apparently, he was drunk most of the time, but the minute he grabbed a scalpel, his fingers stopped trembling and, almost miraculously, he became the finest surgeon in town (actually, he was the only surgeon in town).

The hospital lab extracted some kind of matter from my tonsils, and turned it into a concoction that was injected daily into my body over a period of some weeks. And though I started to improve quite well under that treatment, the doctor felt that I would recuperate much better if I spent several months in a country with a temperate climate, such as South Africa (known in those days as the Union of South Africa).

And, before I knew what hit me, father had enrolled me in a boarding school that was part of the St Joseph College in Rondebosch, South Africa. Rondebosch is a suburb of Cape Town, practically on the south-western tip of the African Continent.

So, here I go again. Another long train ride and another language to cope with. My schooling started with Czech, proceeded in French and now English.

Fortunately, mother unexpectedly decided that she needed a vacation, and that she and Eliska would accompany me to Cape Town. I am convinced, however, that that was an excuse, and that she was actually uneasy about my travelling that far on my own.

Mother's decision made me feel much better about what I was facing. I was not going to travel by myself (for the very first time in my life), and I no longer had to worry about English because there is safety in numbers. I was convinced that, between the two of us, we knew enough of the language to get us by. And so, I truly started looking forward to my next adventure.

The train took three days to reach Cape Town. As it left the Congo, it rolled through Northern Rhodesia and entered Southern Rhodesia via the Zambezi River Bridge, the one that I talked about in my notes about the Victoria Falls. By the way, I should mention again that, when this bridge was built in 1905, it was considered an essential element in the Cape-to-Cairo railroad project, a project vigorously promoted in its time by Cecil Rhodes, the founder of British South Africa. This project is still but a dream.

After crossing Southern Rhodesia, the train proceeded along the eastern portion of South Africa's Bechuland Protectorate (notable for its Kalahari Desert) and finally entered the Union of South Africa proper. It also had the Afrikaans name of Unie van Suid Afrika, a language spoken by the Boers of Dutch descent. Afrikaans is, along with English, an official language of the country. The bulk of the country consists of a vast, inland plain some 4,000 to 6,000 feet above sea level, much of it covered with grass. The South Africans call it the Veld.

This country, which was formalized in 1910 when four autonomous provinces agreed to merge, had its origins in 1652, the year that a Dutch colony took roots in the general vicinity of today's city of Cape Town. The region became a de facto fiefdom of the famous Dutch East India Company that, incidentally, required that all employees and colonists adhere to the Protestant faith.

Worthy of note is the fact that the country has really two capitals. The city of Cape Town, where Parliament holds its sessions, is known as the legislative capital. The Parliament, made up of a Senate and a House of Assembly, is the supreme legislative power of the union. Then there is the city of Pretoria, about 800 miles from Cape Town, where the executive branch of the government holds court. Pretoria is actually the official capital of the Union of South Africa.

During World War ll, Field Marshal Smuts kept the

country on the side of the Allies, despite the leanings of the Boers and their Nationalist Movement. The Boers actually approved of Hitler's "Master Race" theory, and in 1950, when they won the elections, they introduced the repressive racial policies known as Apartheid. These were harsh policies with strict regulations that enforced a complete segregation of the races.

The first South African town that we reached was Mafeking. Then we stopped in Kimberley, about 650 miles northeast of Cape Town. It was established in 1870, only a few short years after diamonds were first found in the area, and now some of the largest diamond mines in the world lie in its vicinity. One of the better-known gemstones, the Hope Diamond, comes from there. The name of the town derives from the word "kimberlite", the mineral that is found deep inside the earth, and happens to be the most important source of diamonds.

Then came Cape Town.

In addition to being the legislative capital of the country, Cape Town is also the capital of the Province of the Cape of Good Hope (usually referred to as the Cape Province), whose coastline stretches from the Indian Ocean to the Atlantic Ocean. The actual Cape of Good Hope, a rocky headland on the Atlantic coast, is an hour's drive from Cape Town. Incidentally, the Cape of Good Hope is not quite the southern-most point of land in Africa. In actual fact, that reputation is held exclusively by Cape Agulhas, about ninety miles to the southeast of Cape Town.

Cape Town, the historical heart of the country, is

wedged between the flat-topped Table Mountain (the town's icon) that is 3,051 feet high, and the blue waters of the Atlantic Ocean. The surroundings are breathtaking and, with its sandy beaches and sunny climate, the city is undeniably the favorite vacation destination of South Africa.

When we arrived in Cape Town, we went on to Muizenberg by a commuter train that links a string of picturesque towns along the east side of the cape peninsula, and travels in the direction of the Cape of Good Hope. One of the communities facing False Bay, is Simon's Town. It is known for its attractive naval base, and for being in the vicinity of Boulders Coastal Park, home to hundreds of African penguins. Those penguins are two feet tall, very curious and well worth the trouble of getting to see them.

Muizenberg, one of Cape Town's five beaches, is a top surf spot, and the water that washes over its beach is reputed to be warmer than anywhere else on the peninsula. The town has a large Jewish community (certain circles call the town Juizenberg), predominantly Dutch style homes, and a lively downtown. I was able to relax there for a whole week, before entering the boarding school. Mother and Eliska left for home several weeks later.

I promptly noticed (very happily I might add) that the discipline in this school was nothing like what I endured in Leopoldville. Everyday life was much less structured and we were even allowed outside the school grounds, without any supervision, on many occasions. However, I went to the beach only when I had a whole day off, because Rondebosch is some distance from the coast, and I was forced to use public transportation to go swimming in the ocean. It was not long before I discovered that the repressive Dutch Reform Church, the semi-official religion of the country, frowned on even the most innocuous of all activities. For instance, one Sunday afternoon, as some of us were planning to race up and down the beach, the police put a quick stop to our fun because racing was prohibited on Sabbath. Also, since the 1945 New Year's Eve holiday extended over a Sunday, we had to wait until the wee hours of Monday morning before going to the movies. No form of public entertainment was allowed to swing into action before midnight that night. By the way, the movie theaters offered more than mere movies. Those places combined restaurant fare with the entertainment of movies, and I quickly became fond of watching movies and eating full-course meals at the same time.

Then, one day I came down with a severe case of chickenpox. I was moved out of the dorm and quarantined in the teachers' residential quarters for quite some time. I do not remember exactly how long the quarantine lasted, but I remember feeling lousy, dejected and rather homesick. And for some reason, the homesickness persisted after I rejoined my classmates. The chickenpox and the isolation had twisted my outlook on life in Rondebosch. I had to do something about this lousy situation but, no matter how hard I tried, I could not come up with something doable.

That was when Harry came to the rescue with a letter that literally sent me into a tailspin. He informed me that the British Bata Shoe Company's College had several openings for the new term, and that he was applying for admission to the two-year course. He wanted to become a Bata Man, just like father. How about myself, was I interested?

Was I interested? What kind of question was that? Who would pass up such a golden opportunity? Who, in his right mind, would not want to join the company and spend two very exciting years in England?

I never wrote a letter as swiftly as the one that implored Father to let me go with Harry.

Of course, Father had no objections, and the destiny of my life was sealed right then and there.

28. Becoming a Bata Man

The train-ride back to Elisabethville turned out to be
far from boring, thanks to my school uniform. I was still
wearing it when I went to the dining car on the first day of
the trip and, while I was involved with my food, I noticed
that four teen-age female students had taken over the next
table. They started to take me apart in French, thinking that
I was a South African on account of my attire, and they really
went at it. I let them have their fun, but as I stood up to leave,
I turned to them and made some racy remark in French.
They became embarrassed, then apologetic and finally quite
friendly. As a result, I enjoyed some very pleasant company
during the whole trip. By the way, same as I, they were
returning to their Congolese homes from a boarding school
in South Africa.

It was good being back, but it seemed that I had hardly
returned before I had to leave again. However, even though
this time I was embarking on a whopper of a trip, I did not
feel any anxiety; I was traveling with Harry.

The first leg of our flight took us from Elisabethville to
Leopoldville. There, in late evening, we boarded another
airplane and flew to Brussels, via Kano, in Nigeria, and
Casablanca, in Morocco. That strenuous night flight seemed
to last forever but, as the darkness dissipated and the sun

appeared on the horizon, we finally reached Kano's airport, where we were given breakfast and the airplane was refueled. The overheated desert air hit us like a cannonball the minute we walked through the airplane's door, and during breakfast we felt as if we were eating in an oven. On the other hand, the layover in Casablanca was very pleasant. This large metropolis, on the Atlantic side of Morocco's coast, looked like a picture postcard from high above, and when we deplaned, the cool ocean breeze that welcomed us was a pleasant change from Kano's broiling heat.

Eventually we landed in Brussels and switched to a commuter flight that took us to our final destination. An employee of the British Bata Shoe Company met us at London's airport, and helped us catch the train for East Tilbury. Before parting, he explained that there were two Tilburys on the rail line, and that we should not panic when, after having stopped in Tilbury, the train backed out of the station, and gave the impression that it was returning to London. But fear not, the next stop would be that of East Tilbury.

When we stepped off the train, we met the principal of the college, and a student who helped with our luggage. We were informed, after the usual handshakes that other foreign students had arrived by an earlier train. Two of them were from Bata Best, the factory in Holland, and the other two from Bata Neuvic, one of the three factories operating in France. With Harry and me, the college would have six freshmen from the company's overseas factories.

The Bata Industrial Training College, known as

B.I.T.C., provided courses in industrial and academic subjects, with particular emphasis on footwear production, and company organization, systems, and procedures. The course in footwear production started off with the study of the foot and its bone structure, proceeded to the design and manufacture of footwear, and went on with an in-depth study of leather and related subjects. The curriculum was so well designed that, at the end of the two years, graduates were ready to handle practically any position, in any Bata company, in any part of the world.

The college was located in a three-story building, right next to the hotel. The students, two to a room, lived on the two top floors of the building. The library, other common rooms, and the residence of the supervisor made up the first floor.

For meals, we went to the hotel's cafeteria, where we were free to eat whatever we wanted. Unfortunately, there was nothing very appetizing about the cuisine. Rationing was still in force, and everything was in short supply. The daily menus offered few choices. Breakfast usually consisted of kippers, lunch fare alternated among a number of sardine platters, and dinner featured various fish concoctions. The ration for meat was so meager that a single portion of ham and eggs utilized a whole week's allotment. After two years of this diet, my aversion to seafood was so strong that I refused to eat fish for a very long time. I could not even look at a fish without losing my appetite.

East Tilbury was a scaled-down Zlin. It had several factory buildings, a hotel, a cinema, a post office, a grocery and low rent housing for the workers. It was set in an agricultural area, a few miles from the Thames River. We often hiked through the fields up to the river, and watched for hours on end the freighters that were heading in and out of London. Because of dredging, even the largest freighters were able to sail all the way to the city docks, some fifty miles from the North Sea.

The college and the factory were on identical schedules. As a result, recess lasted only two weeks, and we could not return home during summer vacation. So, we used up our free time as follows:

The first year we took a train to the town of Henley-on-Thames, where we rented a rowboat, a large tent, and other camping gear. We planned to row up to Oxford, and spend both weeks on the banks of the river. But though we never reached the intended destination because the current turned out to be stronger than expected, the quiet charm of the river, and the hospitality of the people along the way made our vacation worthwhile. I particularly enjoyed the water-locks, and I frequently assisted the lockmaster to man the watertight gates. By the way, four of us were on this camping trip; Harry and I, and the two Neuvic guys.

The following year, we accompanied one of the Dutch students to his home in Malines, near Antwerp. We had become very friendly with him, and his parents graciously invited us to spend our vacation with them. We had a terrific time throughout, but especially on the days that we visited Antwerp. Once, we went to see the port, and boarded the ss Albertville, a sister-ship of the ss Leopoldville, the ocean liner that brought us to Africa in 1939.

During the two years in East Tilbury, we made many day trips to nearby towns, such as Gravesend, Ramsgate, Southend-on-Sea and, of course, the city of London. We never tired of visiting that great metropolis, and I believe that, in the end, we saw everything worth seeing, and witnessed many of the public ceremonies it is so well known for.

I also recall the day we went to a major agricultural Fair that was graced by the presence of King George VI, Queen Consort Elizabeth, and daughters Elizabeth (present Queen Elizabeth II) and Margaret Rose. At one time, Harry and I stood only a couple of feet from the royal family; we were almost close enough to touch them. I was moved by the experience because I regarded them as the giants of our times. During the war years, the royal family became a symbol of Britain's indomitable courage and boundless endurance.

It's funny how time flies when you least expect it to do so. All of a sudden, we had graduated and were flying back to Africa. We were entering a new phase in our lives. We left as students and were returning as full-fledged employees of the Societe Bata Congolaise.

As luck would have it, Father had been transferred back to Leopoldville while we were in England, and when we returned, we moved right back with our family. Father was now in charge of the Bas-Congo and Equateur retail divisions.

Once again, the whole family was together, at least for the time being.

29. Visiting America

When we left Leopoldville and moved to Elizabethville in 1944, the factory compound was located in a remote area, within a distant suburb of the city. When we came back, we found it completely surrounded by a thriving industrial and commercial district that extended from downtown to the N'Dolo Airport. The town itself had changed dramatically. High-rise buildings were going up downtown, in the midst of a large retail zone which included many fine restaurants and several new hotels. The port, with its crisscrossing dock cranes, was a beehive of river trade. Leopoldville was being transformed into a modern cosmopolitan area.

The compound was almost unrecognizable to us. The center roadway and all the lanes were now paved, all buildings were in tip-top shape, and along the water's edge, a massive masonry wall had replaced the ragged contour of the old shoreline (crocodiles could no longer come ashore and sun themselves on the tennis court; what a shame). The big manufacturing complex, with its original tannery, contained individual buildings for the production of leather and rubber footwear, large warehouses for raw materials and finished goods, a workshop for the maintenance and repair of machinery, an infirmary, and a corporate office building. Manufacturing processes were fully mechanized and conveyor-belt systems were used in the workshops.

Because the company was now employing more than a dozen expatriates, most had to live outside the compound. We lived downtown, on the Avenue Charles de Gaulle. But that was only temporary because Father was in the process of building our own home. He had bought a large lot in a new suburb on a high hill overlooking the city. The area was covered with thick vegetation, and monkeys were still jumping among the trees. But, almost as soon as the walls started to climb above the foundations, the Governor General unexpectedly decided to relocate his future residence to that immediate vicinity and overnight the neighborhood became the most desirable residential spot in the city. It was not surprising then that the powerful Banque Du Congo Belge contacted Father about renting the property the moment it became suitable for occupancy. And since it was the president of the bank that desired to move to the house, Father was able to hold out for a top-notch deal on a three-year contract. The bank agreed to a very high monthly rent, forked over two years of rent at the signing of the lease, and started paying off the third year upon receipt of the keys. That large initial payment prompted Father to start immediately on another home for the family - he bought a lot in Kingabwa, an area not yet incorporated by the city, and commissioned an architect to draw the plans for our future house.

Since Harry and I were competent to handle most positions in the company, we were given the jobs of substituting for managers away on home leaves. I was assigned to production, and Harry to retail.

Within a couple of weeks, Harry moved to Elizabethville, where he took over one of the stores, and was put in charge of inventory control at all the other units in town.

I became the assistant manager of the purchasing department and, ultimately, ran the place when the boss went on home leave. I really liked this position because it involved contacting overseas suppliers, negotiating prices, and working with customs agents. In one instance, I took a couple of our company trucks to Matadi to pick up supplies that were critically needed by the workshops. These supplies had been sitting on Matadi's dock for several weeks, and there was no way of knowing when the railroad would move them to Leopoldville. I could not run the risk of halting production, and therefore decided to go and get them myself. Unfortunately, this was the height of the rainy season and, within a couple of hours, one of the trucks sank into the mud up to its axle. I had to spend most of that sweltering night in the truck, eaten up by mosquitoes, while the drivers took off to look for help. They showed up, several hours later, with a dozen men from a distant village and, after a couple hours of hard work, got the truck moving again. We went on to Matadi, cleared the goods through customs, loaded the trucks, and made it back home by the end of that day, almost forty-eight hours after we started on the trip. That was some trip.

When the purchasing manager returned from leave, I became the assistant to the leather production manager and, later on, the rubber production manger. But between these two assignments, Harry and I took our own leaves, and went together to visit our relatives in the U.S.A.

We left Leopoldville in the middle of February (the year was 1952), during the hottest stretch of the summer, and flew to New York via Brussels, Shannon (Ireland), and Gander (Newfoundland), where winter was in full force. The contrast in temperatures hit us hard. However, as though that wasn't bad enough, we also had to endure an extended layover in Gander, in the midst of a violent blizzard. We had landed at the peak of the snowstorm, and a burst of strong wind smashed the door as it was being secured against the fuselage of the airplane. The damage was so bad that a new door had to be ordered from New York. Of course, this meant that the layover would last well over twelve hours, forcing the airline to move us into the airport hotel where we were given warm food and comfortable rooms to collapse in.

We finally landed in New York, and the minute I stepped off the airplane I sensed that I had found my future home. I can not explain it, but that is the way it was.

We spent a whirlwind vacation traveling between New York City, Baltimore in Maryland, Washington DC and Vineland in New Jersey. In New York, we received the red-carpet treatment by Aunt Johanna and Uncle Paul. We went all over Manhattan and saw several Broadway shows. In Baltimore, we were hosted royally by Aunt Olga (her maiden name was Diamant), Uncle Ozzie, and other members of the Bretholtz clan. We visited Washington, and saw some of

Pennsylvania's beautiful countryside.

After Baltimore, we made our way to Vineland, to spend time with Uncle Arnold, Aunt Dora, and Cousin Susanne Balaban and her family. Uncle Arnold and Aunt Dora were living on the poultry farm that I had mentioned in an earlier paragraph. It was a small place, with a one-story farmhouse that sat on a sweeping front lawn, and a couple of chicken coops along the far side of the back yard. Those coops allowed Uncle Arnold to handle ten thousand chickens at a time. He would buy freshly hatched chicks, feed them for fifteen weeks and then auction them through a local cooperative. A couple of weeks later, he would start the process all over again. It was a neat operation.

Cousin Susanne, with husband Max and daughters Miriam, Renee and Eileen also owned a chicken farm. However, that farm produced eggs, not poultry meat, and was more labor intensive than Uncle Arnold's place.

We spent several wonderful days on the farm, helping Uncle Arnold with the chores, watching television (still a novelty for Harry and me) and meeting all their friends. And though Vineland had none of the excitement of large cities, I was surprised how much I enjoyed that wonderful and unhurried rural life-style. As a matter of fact, I even fantasized about living on a farm, and raising chickens.

Once again, I sensed that I was going to come back, and that I was going to spend the rest of my life in this terrific country. Eventually, of course, I did just that.

30. Back On The Job

When we returned home to Leopoldville, I immediately looked into the possibility of transferring to the Bata factory in Belcamp, Maryland, and visited the U. S. Embassy in town to evaluate my chances for an immigration visa to the States.

Management was open-minded about my request for a transfer, but stressed that l had the obligation to fulfill my three-year contract before moving to the U.S.A. The information at the Embassy was also positive. As I was born in Berlin, my visa was subject to the German quota, and since this was altogether an "open" quota, I could expect a visa within a couple of years. In other words, good news all around. I was going to live in the United States, and I was going to make it happen within the next three years.

In the meantime, I went back to assisting the manager in the leather factory, and Harry took over a store in Kamina, one of the towns on the train tracks linking Elisabethville to Port-Francqui.

I had direct supervision of some hundred workers and managed several conveyor production units. Initially, the workers tested me to see if they could take advantage of me, or whether I was up to coping with their annoying tricks. For instance, a worker would deliberately delay production, and lay the blame on his machine. But that nonsense stopped the minute they saw that I was experienced in the ins-and-outs of every position on the conveyor, and could personally operate every single machine on the line.

Once I proved myself, production and quality improved considerably. However, I had a hard time resolving the annoying mystery of vanishing shoes. I posted guards at every door, and made sure that all workers were thoroughly searched as they left the workshop. Nothing helped, and shoes kept disappearing. That went on until a senior guard returned from sick leave, and the personnel department assigned him to my area. Within a couple of days, he dragged one of the workers into my office and, with a toothless grin, pointed to the man's feet. That thief was wearing a pair of shoes branded with the day's production numbers. Evidently, the rascal had the habit of reporting to work in bare feet, and walking out in grand style. It was an original way of stealing, and I was a bit reluctant to turn the man over to the police. The guard received a nice bonus, a bonus that made him flash his toothless grin for days on end.

A couple of months after I returned from the States, my parents and Eliska left on their leave and, all of a sudden, I was alone in the large house on Avenue de Charles De Gaulle. Yes, our house boy George was there to take care of all my needs, but I wanted more than that. I wanted companionship. So, I yielded to my impulse and started looking for a dog, even though I knew that Mother was still against having pets in the family. As I said before, she did not want to go through the heartbreak of losing another pet.

Before long, I learned about a female German Shepherd

that was due to have a litter within days, and I quickly made a down payment toward a male puppy. And, while I waited impatiently for the happy event, I built a large doghouse that had "Zoro" written in bold letters across its entire front. I thought that Zoro was the perfect name for a future German Shepherd champion.

However, when the puppies finally showed up, I was unable to pick a male pup because there were too few of them to go around (I did not have first pick). So, six weeks later, I brought home a beautiful female that had adopted me at first sight. She never left my side and, of course, even slept in my bed. But there was no way that I could call her Zoro, and finally opted for Zora (requiring the change of just one letter on the front of the doghouse).

Needless to say, I stopped feeling lonely the day Zora came to live with me.

It was really wonderful, except that I was apprehensive about the moment when Mother would first lay eyes on our new pet. Finally, I decided that if I kept Zora exclusively outside the house, Mother would not get overly attached to her and that, under the circumstances, would not object to having her around. Therefore, a week or so before my parents were due to return, I started getting Zora used to sleeping in the doghouse. Obviously, that did not go well at first. For a couple of nights she did not sleep at all, and neither did I. Her sad whining was too much to bear. But we both persisted and, by the time my parents came home, all was well on that front.

My parents were rather unhappy with me when they

finally met Zora (Eliska, though, was exhilarated), but they relented when I explained my plan, and mother grudgingly agreed to go along with the status quo. However, in the end, things did not work out as planned.

I came home for lunch one day and, much to my surprise, found Zora relaxing luxuriously on the living room carpet. I took her out at once but, as I walked in from the porch, observed that Mother was looking for her all over the place. In a matter of a few days, Mother had become so attached to Zora, that she allowed her to have the full run of the house. Even George became fond of her. I will always remember the two of them, squatting side by side, watching traffic on the Charles De Gaulle Avenue, while waiting for Eliska to return from school. The bus stop was on the opposite side of the avenue, so that the two of them had to cross over in order to walk her safely across the bustling road.

After my parents returned, and the dust settled down, I started working toward two important goals.

I easily reached the first goal, thanks to father's considerable backing. He helped me finance my first-ever car. It was a brand-new, futuristic-looking, two-door blue Studebaker. That car became my pride and joy, and I maintained it lovingly until I left the Congo.

The second goal was much more arduous. Actually, there were times when I thought that I would never reach it. I wanted to become a bush pilot. The idea came from Harry, who took flying lessons during his assignment in Elizabethville and, though his training was short-lived, could never stop raving about the ecstasy of "soaring through the air". He gave up flying because he was moving around the country too much, and could not maintain a proper training schedule. Instead, he took up photography, and became quite passionate about it. Fortunately, my circumstances were different and, with dogged determination, I eventually earned my pilot's license. And, while I have already written a bit about my flying experiences, more will come later on.

It was around the beginning of my flying days that we moved into our new home, the one that father built after the bank rented the first one. This new home ended up by being totally different from Father's original concept. It became a duplex that Father built in partnership with Monsieur Edward Chvatal, the VP of the company (he was one of the men that had left the Congo to join the Czech army in England, and married his sweetheart Viera when his tank unit liberated his home-town). We had become very good friends with the Chvatals, and living side by side turned out to be a winning move. No one could have been more compatible than our two families. They had three small children, two boys and a girl, and Eliska became their big sister.

The duplex was built outside the city limits, in a wooded area called Kingabwa. It was so far past the city limits that we had no access to utilities. We had a cesspool, a well for water, and a gasoline-powered generator that started on its own whenever there was a call for power. All one had to do, was to turn on a light, for instance, and the generator would start up automatically.

The stucco house had two stories, a multitude of windows for cross ventilation, thick brick walls that insulated against extreme temperatures, very high ceilings and a wide roof-overhang that protected from the sun's direct rays.

Our front door, made of dense mahogany, opened onto a large foyer that doubled as a small parlor. To the left of the foyer, was the living room, dining room and a hallway that led to the kitchen. To the right of the entrance was a powder room and, along the far wall, a sweeping stairway that led to the second floor. That far wall, which had long rows of stylish vertical windows and was two-stories high, gave the foyer a classic elegance, and provided it with abundant natural light. The flight of stairs wound up at a large hall, with access to a centrally located bathroom and three large bedrooms.

At the far end of the property were two "boyeries" (two rooms with a common shower). The house boys lived there during the week, and went back to the black community only when they were given some time off. The gardeners, the laundry boys and the night watchmen commuted on a daily basis.

31. Up In the Sky

The cost of learning to fly was almost entirely subsidized by the government because, in times of crisis, local authorities had to have a ready pool of pilots for emergency sorties into the bush. Obviously, that suited me just fine. I joined the Aero-Club Du Congo Belge, and enrolled in its flight course.

My first flight, supervised by Instructor Bletard, took place on December 3, 1952, in the club's Piper Cub Trainer. It was quite an experience, and I sweated buckets. But I persevered and, after eight hours of supervised training, I progressed to my first solo flight. I lined up carefully at the end of the runway, waited until I received the green light from the control tower (as mentioned earlier, we did not have radios on board), and took off into the wind. I climbed to three hundred meters (some nine hundred feet), circled the airport, turned into the final approach and, once I got another green light, came in for the landing. It was not one of the finest three-point landings on record, but neither was it all that awful. When I emerged from the Cub, I was cheered by a large group of club members who had lined the runway to witness my first solo landing.

After that I flew almost daily since the airport was conveniently located on the road that led from the factory to the Funa Swim Club, and on to our new home in Kingabwa. I usually left work at 4 p.m., went flying for half an hour, and still got to the swim club before 5 p.m. I would play tennis and swim until it was time to rush home for the evening meal. It made for a full schedule, but I loved every minute of it.

With all that, I also had to study for my meteorology, navigation and pilot's exams and, with the assistance of my instructor, go on long-distance flights to master dead reckoning navigation: point-to-point (reference points) navigation. We did not have electronics and had to fly, as I said earlier, by the "seat of our pants". And that was quite tricky at times because there are few convenient reference points (large roads, railroads, etc.) in the bush. In addition, the lush canopy had the nasty tendency to conceal reference points, such as rivers or villages, and gave inexperienced bush pilots a run for their money. As a result, I was cautioned against jumping to rash or careless conclusions and never, but never, presume that a flight was off-course, just because some reference points failed to materialize as expected. Anyway, one of the longest flights that I trained on as navigator was the one to the Air-Rally of Pointe Noire (Rallye Du Mayumbe), French Equatorial Africa (same place where, several years ago, I had vacationed with Mother, Eliska and Harry). The flight took eight hours, and we touched down at seven different airports. I worked hard on filing the flight plan (my instructor handled the border-crossing formalities), plotting the course and making it to our destination without straying off-course. I gained a lot of experience on that trip. Though obviously not enough, as will become clear further on.

At last I became ready to take all the tests for my license.

First came all the written tests. I aced them.

Then came the navigation test. I was to fly from Leopoldville to Matadi, Matadi to Luozi and Luozi back to Leopoldville. I was given four hours to accomplish this circuit, and was expected to land at each checkpoint within a specific estimated time of arrival. Easy enough I thought (I had become rather cocky after my successful navigation run to the Pointe Noire rally), and got ready for the test without much trepidation. I filed my flight plan, studied the latest meteorological data and strapped myself into my faithful Piper Cub, after having completed all the pre-flight checks. I took off, climbed to the appropriate cruising altitude and started looking for reference points. All went well until I got lost. Unbelievably, I had done what I had been warned not to do. I had concluded, rather quickly, that I was off-course because the reference points that I had chosen during pre-flight planning were not turning up under my wings as expected. I decided that the Cub had drifted on a crosswind, and that I had to adjust my heading to compensate for the drift. But the new heading did not help. Well, that turn of events hit me in a physical way (explanation: I became airsick). I had just about time to open the side window, push my head into the slipstream and surrender my breakfast. Luckily, the rush of the slipstream on my face, and the loss of my breakfast, calmed me down, and helped me conquer my panic. I started flying in ever-widening circles until I matched several landmarks with their locations on the map. That showed me where I was, and allowed me to set the proper course to the first checkpoint. I reached it, as well as the other airfields, within the allotted times. So, I passed the test. That day, I also learned a valuable lesson, one that I have never forgotten.

During the pilot's practical test, I had to go through precision landings, stalls, sideslips, et cetera. I do not know why, but I particularly remember the figure-eight circuit. It had to be flown without gain or loss of altitude, and without any skidding (using too much rudder) or slipping (not using enough).

Anyway, I passed all the tests and received my pilot's license on August fourth, 1953. I had fifty hours of flying time in my logbook, and was checked out on the Piper Cub, of course, and the larger Piper Super Cruiser. Eventually, I also flew a Stampe Sw-4 (Gypsy Leopard), a Leopard Moth (open cockpit bi-plane, like Snoopy's Sopwith Camel), and a fully equipped Piper Tripacer that the Aero Club received a few months before I left the Congo.

I never missed an opportunity to take off by myself, and spend as much time as possible in the air. By climbing high, I enjoyed the vast view of the Stanley Pool, and relaxed in the coolness of the altitude. And when it was time to go back, I would drop to a couple thousand feet, sweep low over the fishing villages and make my final approach to the airport.

I flew with passengers the minute I received my license (private pilot license). Mother and Eliska were the very first ones to go up with me. However, shortly after that flight , I started taking bona-fide passengers to various destinations around Leopoldville's extended area. I did this for the love of flying, not for income. Passengers paid the club for all the flight expenses, except for the pilot (only pilots with commercial licenses could demand fees). My rewards consisted of free flight-time, and increased experience in the cockpit.

All my flights were interesting, but as long as I live, I will never forget one in particular. It was the time that I ferried a couple of construction engineers to the Zongo area of the Congo River, where a hydro-electric dam was being built downstream from the Zongo falls. It was a short flight, one that I had flown several times before, but what made this one unforgettable was that I almost crashed during take off from the grass strip. The short landing field was on top of a hill, high above the river, with low-strung electrical wires at the far end of the strip, right where the land dropped abruptly toward the dam's vast construction site. It was not a particularly challenging strip because one could lift-off at a safe distance from the far end, and clear easily the low lying wires (the prevailing winds came from the river, so that I almost always had to take off toward the wires). In any event, as I was about to land on this particular flight, I noticed that the strip had not been kept up for some time, and that the grass was much higher than it should have been. Actually, it was so high that it dragged on the elevators when I made my three-point landing, and stopped the roll within a very short distance. My passengers deplaned, and I taxied to the end of the runway to prepare for takeoff. I expected a long roll because of the tall grass, but I figured that my plane was light enough to overcome the drag of the grass. So, I went to full power and released the brakes. The airplane started to move reluctantly, proceeded to roll at a laggard pace and finally picked up some speed after I managed to lift the tail and free the elevators from the grass' grip. I gained a couple feet of altitude just as I ran out of runway. There was no way to clear those lousy wires or abort the takeoff. The controls were sluggish, which meant that the plane was hardly air-worthy. Any attempt to gain altitude would almost certainly result in a fatal stall. Well, I did the only thing left for me to do. I aimed straight between the wires and the ground, stuck the stick all the way forward, and plunged over the cliff. Once I reached a safe speed, I leveled off, gained the proper altitude and flew home. When I landed, I reported the problem to the control tower and made sure that Zongo remained closed to traffic until proper maintenance made it safe again.

One day I received orders (I was deputized) to pick up a Belgian officer who was on field exercises at some distance from Leopoldville. His father had passed away during the night and the funeral was scheduled for late afternoon. I reached the remote area, and buzzed the dirt strip to locate the small fire that was customarily set when an airplane was expected to come in. The resulting smoke was to help the pilot evaluate the strength and direction of the wind. A native policeman saluted me as I stepped out, and kept the crowd of natives at a safe distance from the craft until we took off. It was a subdued flight all the way back to

Leopoldville.

Unfortunately, as unbelievable as it may be, there was actually one flight that I wished I had never made. It resulted in my license being suspended for a whole month (the withdrawal was hard to take). Anyway, it happened when the company's advertising department asked me to scatter promotional leaflets over the city. I was to make the drop on Sunday, because a huge sales event was set for Monday, and it was thought that this would be the perfect day for the drop. However, flying over the city, I noticed that pedestrian traffic was extremely light and that there was really no point in making the drop. But then I saw a mass of bicycles around a large church and decided to swoop down to scatter the leaflets around the edifice. Unfortunately, the parishioners heard the airplane buzzing overhead and rushed out to see what was going on...essentially ending the celebration of the Mass. By buzzing the church, I had disregarded a very important safety rule (I also made the priest very unhappy). An aircraft can not fly lower than a thousand feet over any city. The priest filed a complaint, and I paid a high price for my foolishness.

As a footnote to this chapter, here is a brief description of the two airports that serve Leopoldville; The N'Dolo Airport, with its 4,429-foot runway, was the only one that was fully operational during my time. It is located close to the center of town and has no room to expand. It is now used for domestic flights. A new airport, one that was completed a couple of years after I left, was built at a considerable distance from town, and was given the name of

the N'Djili International Airport. Its single runway is so long
(it stretches to 15,420 feet) that it is one of the emergency
landing strips for the space shuttle. We were authorized to
use it for touch-and-go practice runs while construction
continued along the perimeter of the field.

32. My Transfer to America

Civil agitation gave the first indication that the colonial lifestyle, the privileged lifestyle that all expatriates were so accustomed to, was about to disappear for good   in his part of the world. The white man became more and more concerned about his future in Africa. The natives were quickly losing their respect for Europeans and, more alarmingly, the authority that was imposed by the colonial power. The most obvious signs of the worsening conditions surfaced when disorders began to erupt around accident scenes. At first, these were only limited disturbances. But as time progressed, they often degenerated into full riots. Many individuals, both black and white, lost their lives before police managed to reach the scene and restore order. This kind of situation would have never, but never, been tolerated in the past. The disorders would have been nipped in the bud, and everyone connected with them would have been thrown in jail. Still, despite all that, life carried on as before, albeit with one marked exception. My official situation had changed. After many years of delays, I had been granted my citizenship, and I was now living in the Congo as a bona-fide Belgian colonist. In the midst of all that, I took over the rubber factory when the manager became ill and flew to Europe for extensive medical treatments. And though

I was up to the task, it was quite challenging in a physical kind of way. For instance, since the molding of sneakers ran around the clock, and I often made surprise inspections to the workshops in the middle of the night, it felt like being on duty twenty four hours a day. Mind you, I never made those late inspections without a couple of guards at my side... As I said before, things were changing. Then, there was the unbearable heat. The roof and the walls of the factory were made of corrugated metal sheets that practically sizzled in the sun and, as if that was not enough, the mixing process and the molding operations continuously disgorged tons of heat into the sweltering environment of the workshops. While I was running the rubber factory, Harry had been transferred from Kamina to Matadi and, on a whim, had decided to get there by an awesome way. Instead of flying, he went by train to Port-Francqui (incidentally, that was the same rail line that brought us to the transit point of Luluabourg, when the family moved from Elisabethville to Lusambo), and then boarded a paddleboat that set course for Leopoldville via the Sankuru, Kasai and Congo rivers. It was a trip to remember, and I regretted not being able to join him on that occasion. However, it made me rethink my trip to the States, and I eventually decided to imitate him in an indirect way. I was going to journey to New York by one of the freighters that steamed up the coast, and called at several African ports, before swinging west and heading toward the U.S.A.

Within months after having moved to Matadi, Harry was urgently reassigned to N'Dolo, because a management post in the leather factory had unexpectedly become vacant, and there was no time to get someone from overseas. However, Harry dearly missed the independent life of a retail manager working far from headquarters, and was unable to get used to all the administrative "nonsense" that he had to endure in his new position. He decided to quit nearly a year later. He gave his notice, left on good terms, and opened his own retail store in the center of Leopoldville. The company gave him a generous line of credit for his operation, and supplied the bulk of the merchandise that he carried in stock. As a matter of fact, his relationship with top management was on such good footing that the company took over the business when he finally left for the U.S.A. in 1958.

I received my U.S. immigration visa during February 1955, and made plans to leave within a couple of months. I finalized my transfer to Belcamp, MD, traded my car for a new Plymouth (to be picked up in Detroit, at GM's Export Division Center), and requested a travel agent to find me a freighter that was scheduled to stop at the most interesting ports along the African coast. Duration of the trip was not important, or so I thought.

Everything seemed to fall into place, until I tried to come up with a departure date. On the one hand, the company was having difficulties getting a replacement from Europe. On the other hand, I was limited by the expiration date on the immigration visa.

In the end, I had to forgo my dreams of exploring the west coast ports, and sailed on a fast freighter that reached

New York only a couple of weeks before the expiration date of the visa. We made one port of call between Matadi and New York. It was either in the Azores, or the Canary Islands. Unfortunately, I can no longer remember which it was.

I left Leopoldville, via the Matadi train, on May 23, 1955. The night before, the Bata expatriates threw a lively party in my honor, and the company presented me with a superb gold watch. The next morning, the whole crowd showed up at the railroad depot for a final send-off.

I boarded the SS Lindy in Matadi, the day before it sailed down river to the port of Boma, where it took on a cargo of bananas, and some other freight. It left port on May 27, 1955, and reached New York on June 12, 1955. There were twelve cabins on board, but only half of them happened to be occupied on this voyage. We were wined and dined throughout the trip, and had the run of the entire vessel. Good food and good company made the time fly. I was 25 years old when I left Africa for my new home, the fascinating U.S.A.

33. First Months In America

Upon arrival in New York, I spent a few days with
Aunt Johanna and Uncle Paul, and the Ellingers (cousin
Ruth, husband Maron and son Allan), and then moved on
to Vineland. I had decided to take three months off before
reporting to Bata Belcamp, and to use Uncle Arnold's and
Aunt Dora's poultry farm as my official address in the States.
I needed this address to apply for a driver's license and to
register at the local draft board (all immigrants, under the
age of 26, were required to do so).

Aunt Dora and Uncle Arnold helped me a lot during
this transitional period in my life (contrary to Harry, I was
not used to living alone) and I will forever remain grateful
to them for welcoming me to their home with such obvious
enthusiasm. The Diamant farm became my first home in the
States.

However, Vineland held another bonus for me, and that
was in the form of Cousin Susanne and her family. True,
I had visited them when Harry and I came to Vineland
in 1952, but that visit was too short for any meaningful
bonding. Anyway, now that I was living there, instead of
passing through, we became very close and quickly made up
for lost time. There was never a dull moment in their home,
and I rarely failed to spend part of each day with them.

The chance of living for the first time among so many relatives, turned out to be a unique and wonderful experience. I immediately realized how incomplete our lives in Africa had been because we had had no personal contacts with relatives over all those years. I decided to change that, and to remain in Vineland for as long as possible (initially, I had thought about traveling around and exploring my new country).

However, I did go on two overnight trips.

First, I went to Detroit, to pick up my new car. I took a bus from Vineland to Philadelphia, where I transferred to the one that took me to my final destination. I spent the night in a Detroit motel and, the following morning, drove in a cab to General Motors. A very efficient customer service agent ran me through the documentation (the packet included a 30-day all-inclusive car insurance, and a road map), and showed me to my car.

I must admit that I did lose my way more than a couple of times, but I made it safely back home without as much as a scratch on my new car.

The second trip took me to Belcamp and Baltimore. I wanted to meet my future bosses and check out Belcamp, the place that was to become my new hometown. In Baltimore, I wanted to visit with the Bretholz clan and spend some time visiting Washington, D.C.

I made it to Belcamp without once losing my way. The meetings went well. I was assigned to the retail section, and instructed to report for work on October 1, 1955. However, I did not like what I observed during my visit. Belcamp

had been built along the bank of the Chesapeake Bay, right
in the middle of nowhere, and was practically devoid of
all city amenities. It was strictly a company village, with
subsidized housing for the workers and a five-story hotel
with a cafeteria, post office, one poor excuse for a cinema
and a tiny variety store. The top floor of the hotel had rooms
with individual bathrooms, at the unbelievable rate of $5.00
per week. I reserved a room in the back, which faced the
Chesapeake Bay, and hoped that the view from the window
would make up, in some way, for the gloominess of the place.

As I mentioned, my first impression of Belcamp was far
from exciting. Nevertheless, I relied on my faithful optimism
to quickly chase away all the apprehensions about this place,
and went on to Baltimore. Aunt Olga and Uncle Ozzi put
me up for the duration of the visit, and made me promise to
spend most weekends with them, once I moved to Belcamp.
What can I say? I was really blessed with wonderful relatives.

My trip back to Vineland was uneventful, and I promptly
resumed the previously established routine. I helped with the
chores at both farms, and even worked with Max when he
decided to paint the outside of the farmhouse.

On one occasion I rented a plane at Vineland's local
airport, and took Miriam and Renee on a long flight over the
whole neighborhood. They got a good kick out of that.

Then came time to report for work, and I left for
Belcamp.

34. Life Interrupted

I reached Belcamp in late afternoon, and proceeded to settle down in my room when I heard a knock at the door. It was my next-door neighbor, Radim Balcar, who had recently come over from Bata Cairo. He introduced himself and invited me to join him for dinner. We went to a restaurant in Aberdeen, some five miles from Belcamp, and spent the evening reminiscing, in French and Czech, about our lives in Africa. This was the onset of a long friendship, and Radim eventually became my best man in 1959 (Harry was my other best man).

We had breakfast in the cafeteria the following morning, and walked to the office where Radim showed me around.

That was how I started my career with the Bata Shoe Company, Inc., Belcamp, Maryland. I remained with the company through the 1980's.

However, to my surprise and great astonishment, that career was almost immediately interrupted by an unexpected turn of events. I received, early in 1956, a bombshell of a "greeting" (it was not the Hallmark type, mind you) from the Selective Service System, which ordered me to report to the Local Board, in Bridgeton, N J, at 7:15 am, on March 16, 1956. I had been drafted, and I was going to spend the next two years in the U.S. Armed Forces.

Yes, I could have decided to go back to Africa, and "saved" two years of my life (two years in the military were two years gone to waste as far as my new job was concerned). And there was also the ironic side of the situation. Joining the military was not even going to speed up the process of my American citizenship. I was still subject to the obligatory waiting period of five long years. However, running away from an obligation would have been inconsistent with my temperament. I had made the decision to live in America and, since this was the price for this great privilege, I was going to foot the bill.

I left Belcamp a few days before my date with the Local Board, and spent that time in Vineland. Uncle Arnold helped me stow the car in the garage, and pack away my meager possessions. The car was lifted off the ground, covered with a tarp, and Uncle Arnold agreed to run the engine at regular intervals.

Then came the longest day of my life. Uncle Arnold drove me to Bridgeton and dropped me off in front of the Local Board's building. Once all the draftees were accounted for, they drove us in a large bus to the Induction Center in Philadelphia, where we were given a series of evaluation tests. We were also asked to indicate which part of the military we wanted to join.

I wrote in capital letters "Air Force" and crossed my fingers!!!

While the tests were being graded, we were given rather disturbing news, as far as I was concerned. It appeared that, contrary to what we had been told earlier, we really had no say about where we would end up, unless we had opted for the navy. The navy, one of the most technical branches of the military, rarely relied on draftees because those men usually left the military the minute their time was up - letting lengthy and expensive training go to waste. However, the navy happened to be in the middle of a grave manpower crisis and temporarily grabbed most of the qualified men that came through the draft pipeline. Hence, all the recruits who averaged over 75% on their tests were going to serve in the navy.

Well, that was exactly what happened to me. Believe me, I did not like it one bit, until I realized that there were pilots in the navy, and that naval stations were located in some of the choicest areas of the States. Who knows, I thought, I might be lucky enough to end up in San Diego, and have the opportunity to see the West Coast. Not for a minute did I think that I would catch sea duty.

We were loaded onto busses and taken to New York City, where the Navy maintained the only Induction Center in the general area. We reached our destination within a couple hours and were finally given the first substantial meal of the day. Unfortunately, that was about the time that I ran into a problem. I needed to go to the lavatory, but I could not find the usual signs for men's restrooms. When I finally had the guts to ask for directions, I learned that the Navy did not have men's rooms, it had "heads" (but heads are at the opposite extremity of the body - where is the logic). That was my first experience with Navy lingo.

Once sworn in, we were put on yet another bus, and

driven to the Naval Training Center in Bainbridge, Md. We finally got there around two in the morning of the following day. I was completely washed out by then, and ready to collapse. The funny part was (although I was not laughing at the time) that I could have walked from Belcamp to Bainbridge, and been there a lot faster. Bainbridge is located on the left bank of the Susquehanna River, only some fifteen miles east of Belcamp.

The next morning started with more forms and a battery of General Classification Tests. GCT is important because it determines a man's future assignment and training; therefore I took this opportunity to write down that I had a private pilot's license and that I was probably qualified for flight training at a naval air center. I was promptly given some new forms to work on, and then taken to another room to be interviewed at length by a commissioned officer. Everything seemed to be going well, until it came out that I was still a Belgian citizen. Sadly, that little detail put a stop to my flying ambitions. Pilots are commissioned officers, and since non-citizens cannot become officers, I was out of luck. Of course, that did not sit too well with me. If I was good enough to be drafted, why was I not good enough for the same opportunities as everyone else? However, in retrospect, it all worked out perfectly well. Had I signed up for eight years in order to become a pilot in the navy, I most certainly would not have met the true love of my life.

The real fun started right after the tests-crew cuts (required weekly during basic training), thorough medical examination (including "Operation-Pin-Cushion," when both upper arms were injected at the same time while one walked between two corpsmen), clothing issue, and so on.

I was assigned to Company 124 and, carrying a sea bag crammed with the newly issued gear, was marched with eighty other men to our company barrack.

Familiarization with ship terminology started the minute we walked inside. A wall was a bulkhead, stairs were ladders, the floor was the deck and the entrance area was the quarterdeck. We had entered a brand new world, and our daily lives were now under the permanent control of the Company Commander.

Training was hard, the hours were long, and the discipline was tough. Nevertheless, the nine weeks of basic training eventually drew to a merciful end, and all of a sudden we were preparing for our graduation day! It turned out to be a glorious day, full of military pomp and circumstance, fully enjoyed by a large attendance of relatives and friends. Uncle Arnold and Aunt Dora were at the ceremonies, as well as Aunt Johanna, Ruth and Allan, and Miriam and Renee. Before leaving at the end of that wonderful day, Uncle Arnold promised to pick me up the minute I received the two-week leave that was customarily given to newly graduated seamen (I was no longer a "seaman apprentice"). He was not going to let me waste a whole day on a bus trip to Vineland.

I was more than ready to leave Bainbridge for good, and spend a couple of weeks of "freedom" among relatives. But I was also eagerly awaiting my orders, and keeping my fingers crossed for an interesting posting.

However, when the orders finally came, I was stupefied by what I got. No, I was not being posted to a West Coast station (my ultimate wish), or another Naval Base for that matter. Instead, I got what I least expected. I caught sea duty. I was ordered to report to the U.S. Naval Receiving Station in Norfolk, VA, where I was to await sea transfer to the U.S.S. Salem, CA-139. This vessel, a heavy cruiser, was at the time on a prolonged cruise in the Mediterranean, where it had been deployed as the Flagship of the Sixth Fleet. And when I inquired about the meaning of "prolonged cruise", I was informed that, although overseas deployments ordinarily lasted an average of six months, the Salem was scheduled to remain on continuous duty in the Mediterranean for over a year and a half.

What lousy luck was that? Not only was I going to be unable to travel across the States, compliments of the navy, I was actually going to be stuck outside the States for over a year! I had drawn duty on the only vessel in the navy that was on a "prolonged cruise". My rotten luck started when I could not go to flight training, and now this. It was like adding insult to injury.

Once again, though, my optimism helped me get over the initial jolt, and I started thinking that maybe, just maybe, duty in the Mediterranean might turn out to be a winner. After all, who has not heard about the charms of the Riviera?

I spent two leisurely weeks in Vineland and, after a lengthy bus ride, reported to the Naval Station in Norfolk.

Boy that was one huge base. It had all the bells and whistles of a military facility, plus the bustle of a large port.

It had all kinds of vessels tied alongside its docks, and I spent hours walking around the port area. I had no real duty, and was on my own most of the time. I even went swimming at nearby Virginia Beach. Under these circumstances, the long wait for our departure was easy to endure. I was part of a group of some fifty sailors being transferred to various ships in the Sixth Fleet.

We finally left for the Mediterranean in the early evening of June 28, 1956, on board the U.S.S. Oglethorpe. After boarding, we were given a few minutes to store our gear, and then mustered on deck for briefing and job assignments. I was picked for the mess-cooking detail, and was advised to hit the bunk because my shift was scheduled to start at four am.

I reached the galley just before four, drowsy and wobbly on my feet, and was led to a deep fryer where I was to cook spuds for the breakfast crowd. The deep fryer was a big tub full of boiling oil that lurched from side to side, in unison with the swaying ship. In no time at all I started feeling a little woozy. The odor of frying spuds, at four in the morning, was quite unpleasant and overwhelming. That acrid odor, combined with the constant motion of the lurching oil and the unpleasant roll of the ship, hit me all of a sudden with a terrible attack of seasickness. I rushed topside, hung over the handrail, and heaved pitifully over the side of the ship. Fortunately, thanks to the Chief who came looking for me with a pack of dry saltine crackers, I got gradually better and eventually returned to the galley. Wisely though, I kept far away from the deep fryer and happily scrubbed pots and pans for the rest of the trip across the Atlantic.

The crossing took some two weeks, and on July 14, 1956, I finally laid eyes on the Salem. It was moored to its buoy outside the port area of Villefranche-Sur-Mer, a small fishing village a few miles east of Nice, in close proximity to Antibes, Cannes, Monte Carlo, and other unique villages sandwiched between the Maritime Alps and the sea coast. This was the ship's "home port" for the duration of its Mediterranean cruise, and I realized instantly that there could be no nicer home-away-from-home in the whole universe!

Charles II, Duke of Anjou, built Villefranche at the end of the 13th century as a "free port". The medieval fishing port's Old Town section has cobbled streets and pastel-shaded houses. The sheer slopes that surround the harbor, and the twisting streets and steep stairs that hurtle down towards the port give the place the look of an ancient amphitheater.

35. The Navy

A couple of launches brought us from Villefranche's fleet landing to the accommodation ladder on the port side of the ship. We climbed on deck and, after a few words of welcome by the duty officer, were moved to the mess hall for briefings and duty assignments.

First we were given some information about the ship, its current mission and the nuts and bolts of life on board.

The Commander of the Sixth Fleet, Vice Admiral Charles R. Brown, had chosen the U.S.S. Salem for his permanent Flagship, and had moved on board with his entire staff. The ship functioned as a good will emissary to the many countries it visited and, as such, was constantly on the go between all the major ports that surround the Mediterranean basin.

Together with Flag's personnel, the Salem had a crew of 1,500 men, and yet was totally independent of local sources of supply. It was re-supplied monthly by Sixth Fleet Service Force vessels that brought everything from depots in the States. The Salem received those supplies by highlines and fueling booms, while the ships sailed side-by-side on the open sea.

And though this briefing went on for some time, I can no longer recall what else was passed along to us. Anyway, it finally ended when our assignments were handed down and we were taken to our respective divisions. For me, that was the Fox Division.

The Fox Division was the largest division aboard. Its primary function was to operate the ship's complex fire-control equipment and to ensure that this equipment was constantly at peak performance (in this context, "fire-control" refers to the electronic guidance and control of heavy guns). Administratively, Fox Division was divided into three groups, or batteries; three-inch, five-inch and eight-inch. I became a member of the five-inch group.

As would be expected, training played an important role in the daily activities of the division's personnel. Lectures, films and on-the-job repair work perfected our skills and helped us cope with the intricacies of the equipment. We were also encouraged to sign up for correspondence courses and were told that doing so would enhance our chances for early promotions. But then we were also informed that it took usually two years of practical experience and intensive study, to turn a new recruit into the lowest ranked petty officer... What kind of incentive was that for a two-year man?

Once more, I did not get discouraged. I just knew that there was a way to make it happen faster. I studied hard, and never missed a chance to train on the equipment. And that was how I reached the rank of petty officer, third class, in about a year.

I became a Fire Control Technician, Third Class (A), on June 16, 1957, while the Salem was docked in Palma, the major port on the Spanish island of Majorca. The certificate validating my new rank was handed to me by our commanding officer, Captain F. T. Williamson, during a brief ceremony on the fantail deck of our ship. It was truly a memorable day, made more so by an extended liberty in Palma.

As I mentioned earlier, I was assigned to the five-inch battery-control group, and eventually became responsible for the maintenance at one of the two "skies" on board. A "sky" is a steel booth, on top of a tower, that is made to rotate 360 degrees. It has a radar antenna on the roof that moves vertically, and a radar console that is connected to the plotting room. It holds four men; an officer that is in charge, one man who controls the vertical movement of the antenna, one who handles the rotation of the "sky", and one who operates the radar. The radar operator was yours truly. Our job was to "lock" on an intruder by rotating the sky and adjusting the position of the antenna until the intruder's electronic signal merged with the center of the crosshairs on my scope. That was when I pressed a knob and started the locking phase of the radar. Once that phase started, the "sky" and the antenna automatically followed all of the intruder's moves, no matter how evasive they were. The changing coordinates flowed continuously to the plotting room, where powerful computers crunched them with additional data, such as the parallax angles, the wind's strength and direction, and the speed and heading of the ship. And it took only seconds for respective firing solutions to flow directly to the five-inch guns. The system was so good that the guns hit over ninety percent of their targets.

In addition to my "sky" duty, I had two other assignments;

The first one involved standing watch on the bridge. It was stressful and rather tedious, especially in the wee hours of a mid-watch. I did not relish that task.

But the other assignment was quite the opposite. It came with perks that were so outstanding that, at first, I could not believe my good fortune. I became the ship's interpreter, and my main duty was to be the liaison between the shore patrol and the local police, whenever we visited a French speaking country.

As perks go, nothing gets better than being one of the first sailors to leave the ship upon return to Villefranche, and living ashore for as long as we remained in our homeport. Also, since I was acting in an official capacity, I was given per-diem allowances that paid for decent hotel rooms and all meals. Let me tell you, that felt like heaven on earth, especially after a long cruise on the open sea.

Believe it or not, even that got better, given that I had to report to the local police station only every other day, for eight short hours of duty with the shore patrol. My shifts went from 1400 hours to 2200 hours military time (from 2pm. to 10pm, for the uninitiated), leaving me totally free for a day and a half.

I was also issued an ID card that made it legal for me to wear civilian clothes during off-duty hours. As a result, I spent most of my time like a genuine tourist, and even frequented the Monte Carlo Casino, which was strictly off limits to military personnel in uniform.

I should point out one more perk that I enjoyed as a result of my unique duty. I was able to escape most of the Captain's Inspections, and all the drag that goes with this age-old naval custom. Captain's Inspections were held when we were in a port, mostly on Saturday mornings.

Many interesting incidents occurred while I was on duty with the shore patrol.

One evening, an old woman burst into the Nice police station and told me that a bunch of burly sailors roughed her up in an alley, and that her teeth were lost in the melee. She wanted money for a new set of dentures. I explained her demand to the lieutenant, and voiced my firm conviction that the woman was lying (I could not believe that any of our men were "desperate" enough to attack the likes of her). Furthermore, her mouth did not appear to have ever had dentures in the past. Nevertheless, he decided to give her the money because he did not want to tarnish the Navy's public image.

In Beirut, Lebanon, we had untold problems with pickpocket incidents. Street kids would crowd around a sailor and, after having expertly slit his back pocket with a razor, would run away with his wallet, while he was left yelling and clutching the wound on his buttocks. Those kids were accomplished muggers, and all the police could do, was take the victim to Beirut's main police station, where the Shore Patrol corpsman dressed his wound, and I helped him file a report with the detectives. Because the corpsman and I worked on so many of those events, we became fairly friendly with one of the detectives, who eventually invited us to a meal at his home. The food was good, but I became rather thirsty because most of it was also very hot (and I do not mean temperature-wise; I mean as in Spicy, with a capital "S"). So, instead of reaching for my cup of tea, I grabbed a bottle of water and filled my glass to the rim. While doing so, I noticed that the detective was observing me with something of a worried look on his face, but I still drank most of the clear liquid in one big swig because my mouth was really on fire. I immediately felt as if I had been struck by lightning, and hurtled through the roof. That was not water that I had gulped down, it was a very potent alcoholic drink favored by the local population. It may have been something called Arak, fermented palm liquor. The guests had a good laugh at my distress, and I had to endure a long pause before the room stopped moving around.

In the port of Split, Yugoslavia (Croatia, today), I was asked to help the supply officer decide about the safety of some fresh vegetables that had been brought over by a local farmer (once in a while, the ship used local produce). By using Czech, I was able to determine that human waste had been used as fertilizer on the field. Well, the farmer was paid for his produce, but we did not use it. The supply officer had it all thrown overboard once we left port.

Let me tell you, life was not boring during this period of my military service.

36. Life of a Sailor

Life on board ship was structured, of course, but relatively easy, despite the total lack of privacy. Chow was good and plentiful, and the daily routine was only occasionally interrupted by General Quarters and firing exercises. Once in a while, the ship would stop dead in the water and we would be allowed to dive overboard into the warm Mediterranean sea. Swimming was fun, but the climb up the long Jacob's Ladder was tedious at best (guards, with rifles at the ready, stood watch for sharks). The crew was also encouraged to tackle hobbies. I took up photography, like Harry had done some years earlier, and learned to develop my own films. World news was published in the Witch's Brew, the Salem's daily newsletter.

Because Salem was the Fleet Flagship, it hosted a number of high-ranking NATO officials, and political personalities, such as President Truman, the Shah of Iran, President Chamoun of Lebanon, Secretary of the Navy Thomas and several United States Senators.

As I said before, we sailed into innumerable ports in the Mediterranean region, and were always given ample time ashore. Every port was unique, and I enjoyed all of them to the fullest. Before each landfall, the ship printed pamphlets that gave vital information about the port; such as currency, points of interest, restaurants, nightclubs, out-of-bound areas, et cetera.

Aside from the liberties that we enjoyed in all the ports of call, we were given remarkable opportunities to visit major inland cities. These trips, organized by American Express, were well priced for a sailor's pocketbook. For a mere $55.00, I was able to spend three full days in Paris, and that price included the rail trip from Nice to Paris, the hotel and all meals (even a visit to the Moulin Rouge). I also went on a trip to Rome, during the Salem's stop-over in Genoa, and had the unique opportunity of seeing Pope Pius XII at an audience in his summer residence, the imposing Castle Gandolfo. As with Paris, I saw the highlights of Rome, including the Sistine Chapel and Vatican's great museum (its wealth, in jewels and lumps of gold alone, is unimaginable).

By the way, the days spent touring with American Express, were not deducted from our yearly leaves, and that perk allowed me to save an entire week for my parents' visit, when they came to Nice with Eliska, in the Fall of 1958.

But, before I tell you more about this visit, let me comment on some of the ports of call which, for one reason or another, have come to mind.

The beautiful island of Majorca was outstanding, as far as I am concerned, for two reasons. First, of course, because it was the place where I received my Petty Officer's stripes, and then because Frederic Francois Chopin (1810-1849) the great Polish pianist and composer, lived there with his lady friend, the French novelist George Sand, in the mid 1830's. Unfortunately for the world, a quarrel ended their ten-year friendship, and caused Chopin to stop composing music for the rest of his life. I saw the house where they lived until Sand left Chopin and returned to Paris.

Our visits to Piraeus, Athens' port, meant a lot to me. In school I had learned a great deal about ancient Greece, and had always been fascinated by its history. After all, Athens' ancient traditions, culture and code of laws, have positively impacted the civilization of the western world for over two thousand years. Now, thanks to the Navy, I was given the opportunity to walk among the places that I knew from my history books. I will never forget the magnificent temples of the Acropolis, some of the most beautiful buildings in the world. What a tragedy that the center portion of the Parthenon was wrecked in 1687, when the Turks used it as a powder house.

We reached Istanbul, the largest city in Turkey, through the important waterway that leads from the Aegean Sea to the land-locked Black Sea. We sailed through the strait of Dardanelles, into the Sea of Marmara and finally dropped anchor at the southern entrance to the Strait of Bosporus. A strong undercurrent flows east through the Bosporus, and carries salty water into the Black Sea, which would otherwise be a fresh-water body. That current is so powerful that rope nettings were rigged under the gangway ladder to protect us from being swept away if we fell accidentally in the water. Istanbul stretches over two continents, across the Bosporus, Europe is on the left bank, and Asia Minor on the right. It is one of the oldest cities of the world and, for over 1600 years, was known as Constantinople. It was renamed Istanbul in

1929. By the way, when first built, it stood on seven hills, just as Rome. Though modern, it also retains much of the charm from its past, such as the Grand Bazaar, where some three thousand shops offer everything under the sun, from nuts to antiques. The beautiful Blue Mosque, actually the Sultan Ahmet Mosque, was built in 1610, and is unique because of the magnificent blue tiles that cover the walls, and its six minarets (it is the only mosque in the world with so many minarets). As I walked in, I was taken by surprise when I saw a group of young boys, with head covers, swaying back and forth while chanting the Koran (like young Jewish boys studying the Torah). It was as though I was standing inside a synagogue. I also have a very pleasant memory of lunching at the Hilton Hotel. The shish kebab meal concluded with cups of strong Turkish coffee freshly brewed at the table by a waitress in colorful harem clothes. She arrived with a cart full of coffee paraphernalia and performed a whole ritual before finally pouring the aromatic brew into our cups. The oversized dining room windows overlooked the Bosporus, and the bustle of the water traffic added to the enjoyment of the meal.

On one of our visits to Valletta, on the island of Malta, we remained in port longer than was usual (except Villefranche, of course), because the Salem had to go into dry docks. Valetta was chosen for the job on the merits of its vast dockyards, and its long expertise in repairing and refitting the warships of the British Mediterranean fleet. The island of Malta, with its four near-by islands, some sixty miles south of Sicily, is a tourist's heaven and a place of great historical interest. The island's large limestone caves have yielded a treasure-trove of material that helped archaeologists recreate the past. They even found relics of Phoenicians who colonized the island many hundreds of years before the Christian era. They arrived from the coastal region of today's Syria and, while they were great sailors, they were also highly accomplished craftsmen who have been credited with the discovery of glass. English or Italian is used for business, but most of the local people use the Maltese language, which is a mixture of Arabic and Italian.

In Genoa, an important Italian port, I visited the modest house where Christopher Columbus is supposed to have been born. It is close to the Doge's Palace, in the vicinity of the Piazza De Ferrari, the center of this hilly city. I also wandered through the famous cemetery of Staglieno, renowned for its elaborate graves and fine statuary. One of the graves has a statuette that is said to be an exact rendering of the bag lady who is buried there. This woman lived all her life on city streets to save enough money for that marble memorial.

Venice, the queen of the Adriatic, is one of the most famous and remarkable towns on the globe. We anchored in the Grand Canal, a stone's throw from San Marco Square, and the hub of city life. This square is paved with trachyte and marble, and is striking evidence of Venice's ancient glory. It is enclosed on three sides by symmetrical colonnades, and on the fourth by the fabulous San Marco church. The roof is a great cluster of golden domes, and the whole structure is adorned with 500 columns of rare oriental marble. This is considered the greatest example of Byzantine art and architecture. Directly across from the square, over an archway, is the Torre Dell Orologio, with its famous trick-clock. Two bronze giants, each armed with a mallet, strike the hours on a large bell. It was erected in 1497. The canals with their boats and gondolas give this unique city an exceptional charm and a distinct beauty. I fell in love with her.

37. The Missing Salem

Father was able to organize the last family leave (last leave before his retirement) around the time that the Salem was scheduled to return to Villefranche for one of our extended homecomings. Father mother and Eliska flew directly from Leopoldville to Nice, and checked in at the fancy Negresco Hotel. Actually, I moved there as well since I was on my regular Shore Patrol duty, and father footed the bill for my room (there was no way that my lodging allowance could have even remotely covered the rates charged by Negresco). And so, it turned out that we spent a lot of time together, even before the start of my leave.

One day the Salem held an open house and I brought my family on board for a private tour. The ship was dressed up in its formal canvas, with multicolored pennants flying from bow to stern. It was a sight to behold and I was very proud of being one of the crew. The tour impressed them, but the climax came when we went through the mess hall. Father almost keeled over when he saw the variety, quality and profusion of food that had been prepared for lunch. That "feast" (his own word) triggered a flashback in his mind and he could not stop talking about the pathetic rations that he endured during his years in military service. He got a cup of black coffee and a stale roll for breakfast, a weak broth with a dry bread for lunch and some bland concoction of potatoes and meat for dinner.

The minute my leave started, Father rented a car and we drove to Eze, a village perched at the top of a pyramid-shaped rock that rises over 1,000 ft above the sea. And, as if that was not grandiose enough, there is, in its immediate vicinity, an exotic garden that adds to the extraordinary charm of the entire area. My parents intended to vacation in Eze for a couple of weeks, then visit Vienna and other cities in Europe, before returning to the Congo for the last time. But Eliska was not going to leave with them. She was going to attend the Institution Chateau Mount-Choisi in Lausanne, Switzerland, before rejoining our parents in Leopoldville, for their final year in Africa. At the end of that year they were expected to leave Congo for good.

Father's plans were to retire from Bata Congo in January 1959, and move the family to Brussels, Belgium, into a large apartment with a minimum of three bedrooms. Our parents and Eliska would occupy two of the bedrooms, and Harry or I would use the third one whenever we came for a visit. But father did not think, for one minute, about a "full" retirement. He had worked all his life and could not see himself lying around and doing nothing. He had already mentioned this to several Bata people in Brussels, and was convinced that something worthwhile would come his way at the right time.

The other thing that father discussed during our walks around Eze, was the matter of the houses the family owned in Leopoldville. He wanted to leave one villa to each one of

us and, since there were only two of them at the time, he was
going to build a third one in the Parc Yolo area of Limete,
a new residential suburb of town. The architect's plans were
ready, and building was to start the minute he returned to
Leopoldville.

My week in Eze flew by, and suddenly it was time for
me to rejoin the Salem. It was hard to say good-bye, and
leave my parents and Eliska behind. But duty called, and I
had no choice in the matter.

I was kind of depressed during the bus ride, and became
outright gloomy when I realized that I had misplaced the
Salem! Of course, it was none of my doing but, just the same,
the Salem was nowhere to be seen. The bus had rounded a
hairpin bend on the Middle Corniche, revealing the coast
and Villefranche, but nothing else. To my dismay, there was
only empty water where the Salem should have been moored
to its buoy.

I knew right away that something odd must have
happened in the last couple of days, and that I had not heard
about it because Eze was in such a remote area.

I thought about my next move, and decided to report to
the American Consulate in Nice. One of their officials acted
as a military attache, and would surely know what to do with
me. When I got there, I was informed that the Sixth Fleet
had suddenly left for the strife-torn Middle East, and that all
sailors stranded ashore were going to be flown back to their
vessels within the next twenty four hours. However, when
I asked about our destination, I was told, in no uncertain
terms, that this was classified information and that all I

needed to be concerned about was to be at the Nice airport by 0800 hours, the following morning.

I walked out of the Consulate, went to the nearest bar and questioned the waitresses about the location of the Salem. The answer came quickly and without hesitation. The Salem had pulled into Naples to wait for its missing men, and was expected to resume its run to the Middle East the minute every one was accounted for. The ongoing emergency had something to do with England, France and Israel attacking the Sueze Canal.

The following morning, we boarded a navy plane that had taken off from Paris with a bunch of stranded sailors, and was now on the way to Naples. Yes, the barmaid had the right scoop. The Salem was indeed in Naples. I guess the whole world knew about Naples, except the sailors trying to rejoin our ship. That does not say much about "classified" information, does it?

We rushed at flank speed toward Egypt, and spent over thirty days circling the volatile area. We basically blocked the French and English navies from bombarding Egyptian targets. The strategy worked well. The naval situation was neutralized and, having accomplished our mission, we returned to Villefranche for some well-deserved rest and recreation.

And then I received some fabulous news. The navy was cutting short the active duty of the draftees it had deployed overseas, such as myself, and was preparing to transfer them back home by the first available transport. Those on the Salem were going to leave the ship in the next port of call, namely Lisbon, Portugal.

I left the Salem on Friday morning, August 9, 1957, and was flown with the other lucky sailors, from Lisbon to Port Lyautey, a major US Naval Air Station in Morocco. The base is located on the Sebou River, near the Atlantic Ocean, alongside the road that runs between the capital city of Rabat and the coastal city of Tangier. It used to be a French Military Fort, but had been taken over by the U.S. during World War II.

About a week later we heard that we were going to be bussed to Casablanca over the night of the 19th, to await the MSTS General Leroy Eltinge, which was expected to make port early the following morning.

The Eltinge had brought Turkish troops from South Korea to Istanbul (they had fought valiantly during the Korean conflict), and was currently on its way to New York. She was not the HMS Queen Mary, but to us she was one of the most beautiful vessels of the world; she was taking us back home. We looked forward to a pleasurable crossing of the Atlantic. Sadly, we quickly discovered that the chow left a lot to be desired. The Elroy had not been resupplied after its long voyage to Turkey, and some of the meager provisions on board had actually gone bad. But in the end none of that mattered, we were on our way back to the good old USA.

The crossing was uneventful. We arrived at the U.S. Naval Receiving Station in Brooklyn, on August 28, 1957. I was back home 14 months, to the day, after having left Norfolk on the SS Oglethorpe. I was thrilled about being back, and could hardly wait to resume civilian life. Unfortunately, the Navy needed over four weeks to complete all the formalities, and it was only on October 2, 1957, that I was formally released from active duty. However, I remained on reserve duty for four additional years. My Honorable Discharge was issued on March 1962.

From Brooklyn, I went to Vineland for a couple of weeks of R & R, and then returned to Belcamp and my career at Bata. Imagine my surprise when I ran into Fred Kon (the same Fred that I knew in Leopoldville) as I walked into the office that first day. He had moved to Belcamp and had taken over the company's import/export division. I went to work for Fred right then and there, and subsequently became his assistant manager. I became the manager of the division after Fred was promoted to the higher position of marketing manager of all the sales divisions in Belcamp (my experience at running the purchasing department in N'Dolo came in handy). We imported footwear mainly from Bata's overseas factories, but when the need arose, also purchased merchandise from other foreign resources. The bulk of our imports came from Bata factories in India, Sri Lanka, Pakistan, Malaysia, Singapore and France. Non-Bata merchandise came from Japan, Taiwan, South Korea and Hong Kong. The building of lines, quality control and price negotiations required personal supervision, and forced me to travel extensively to that part of the world.

38. Our Wedding

Harry immigrated to the USA mid 1958, and landed a position in the footwear department in Macy's store on 34th street in New York City. Actually, he got this job through a series of interventions. I called the Bata representative in New York City and he, in turn, called one of the Macy shoe buyers that he knew very well (Macy did volume business with us). The buyer contacted their personnel department (called human resources department in todays' business world) and made sure that Harry was hired on the spot. Once again, Harry and I were living relatively close to each other. We saw each other very often.

Then, another wonderful thing happened. I met Leila, the future love of my life, through the undaunted efforts of Aunt Dora. She wanted to see me hitched in the worst way, and usually had a blind date lined up for me whenever I came to Vineland. But since none of them showed any results, she decided, in her infinite wisdom, to turn to reverse psychology. One evening, while we were having dinner, she pointed out to Uncle Arnold that Mrs. Roseman's fashion show in Atlantic City had been a huge success (Aunt Dora shopped in Mrs. Roseman's store). Then, she proceeded to add, as an after-thought (oh, she was so cunning), that Mrs. Roseman's daughter was by far the prettiest of all the models in the entire show. I immediately asked why she had failed to mention in the past this attractive lass, and asked whether she could do something about this terrible omission, right then and there. Her answer was a crafty " I really did not think that you would be interested. But OK, I will see what I can do".

Aunt Dora placed the call, and I was able to visit with Leila over the phone, before heading back to Belcamp (this was late on a Sunday night). We chatted at length, until I finally worked up enough courage to ask for a date on the following weekend. The rest is history. We met for the first time that particular weekend (July 4th, 1958) and married eight months later, on March 15th, 1959.

In the meantime, Eliska had left Lausanne for Leopoldville, where our parents had taken residence in a sixth floor apartment of a high-rise building. Civil disorders were on the rise, and father had decided to make the move because the center of the city was safer than the distant neighborhood of Kingabwa.

Many years later, Eliska had this to say about some of the events that happened during her last months in Africa. And I quote:

> *"One Sunday afternoon, I went to a matinee with a boy friend and, as luck would have it, decided to come home right after the movie. What we did not know at the time, was that new disturbances had erupted in the Cite, and that the fighting was moving to the outskirts of Leopoldville. The next morning, since our boy George did not report for work at the usual time, mother decided to take Zora on her*

*morning walk. As she entered the hallway, she came upon
a number of Europeans who had hidden overnight in the
building, to escape the intense fighting on the streets. We had
been insulated in our sixth floor apartment and had no clue as
to what was happening outside. After that, father decided to
take the family out of Leopoldville altogether, and to move us
temporarily to an apartment in Brazzaville. He also convinced
the company to do likewise with the other dependents of its
European employees, for as long as the danger persisted. It
may be strange, but I do not remember being afraid. I know
this was rather illogical, but believe that it was due to the
fact that everything was happening so fast. I had no time to
dwell on anything. At any rate, father retired on February
13, 1959, and we flew from Brazzaville to Nice, where we
met with Cecile and Roger Diamant (French cousins living
in Paris). We stayed with them a couple of weeks, and then
flew to the States for Henri's and Leila's wedding. There was
no point going first to Brussels because our household goods
were still in transit and mother was not eager to move into a
sparely furnished apartment. Accordingly, we had more time
in the States than originally intended and got well acquainted
with Leila and her parents, Minnie and Charles Roseman,
before the wedding".*

Ah, our wedding. Well, although the suspense was
intense and time dragged on, the enchanting date of
March 15, 1959 finally came around and, despite the fact
that it rained cats and dogs, it turned out to be the most
memorable day of my life. We tied the knot in an attractive
hall downtown Philadelphia, in the presence of some one

hundred and fifty friends and family members. Overseas guests, such as the Chvatals, who could not make the trip, dispatched congratulatory telegrams that were read over the hall's loudspeakers during the course of the reception. Eliska and Dolores Hall were Leila's maids of honor, while Harry and Radim Balzar were my best men. And though I was in a fog most of the time, I still remember the deep emotion that gripped me when I heard the Rabbi pronounce us husband and wife. After all the hoopla ended, we changed clothes and drove to a hotel near the Idlewild Airport in New York, now renamed Kennedy Airport, where we spent the night. The next morning we flew to the beautiful and sunny island of Bermuda for a week-long honeymoon. Several days later, Mother, Father and Eliska flew to Brussels and their new life away from Africa.

After some twenty years, our family was suddenly left with no direct ties to Africa... The Africa that we had escaped to... The Africa where Eliska was born... The Africa that held so many memories... That was the end of a remarkable era for us all.

Acknowledgments

I am greatly indebted to my wife Leila, and my daughter Michele, for helping me whenever I reached an impasse with some phraseology, and for unselfishly putting up with me whenever I became obsessed with this work, and failed to give them the attention they rightfully deserved.

Many thanks to my brother Harry, sister Eliska, as well as cousins Susanne Balaban and Ruth Ellinger, for their help and advice.

Last but not least, I want to acknowledge the invaluable guidance that I received from my cousin Helene Jawer and good friend Paula Mathai.

Glossary

Colonial-Era Names	Current Names
Elisabethville	Lubmbashi
Jadotville	Likasi
Leopoldville	Kinshasa
Livingstone Rapids	Boyoma Falls
Luluabourg	Kananga
Port-Francqui	Llebo
Stanley Pool	Malebo Pool
Stanleyville	Kisangani

Epilogue

Our mother passed away on April 6th, 1961. She is buried in the Kraainem Cemetery, in Brussels, Belgium.

Harry married his wife Mally in Las Vegas, Nevada, in April, 1962, They have two daughters, Renee and Judy.

Eliska was married to her husband Leon Schipper in Baltimore, Maryland, in September, 1962. They have two sons, Gerard and Kenneth.

Our father passed away on November 11th, 1972. He is buried in the Eden Memorial Park Cemetery, in Mission Hills, California.

The future of publishing...today!

Apprentice House is the country's only campus-based, student-staffed book publishing company. Directed by professors and industry professionals, it is a nonprofit activity of the Communication Department at Loyola University Maryland.

Using state-of-the-art technology and an experiential learning model of education, Apprentice House publishes books in untraditional ways. This dual responsibility as publishers and educators creates an unprecedented collaborative environment among faculty and students, while teaching tomorrow's editors, designers, and marketers.

Outside of class, progress on book projects is carried forth by the AH Book Publishing Club, a co-curricular campus organization supported by Loyola University Maryland's Office of Student Activities.

Eclectic and provocative, Apprentice House titles intend to entertain as well as spark dialogue on a variety of topics. Financial contributions to sustain the press's work are welcomed. Contributions are tax deductible to the fullest extent allowed by the IRS.

To learn more about Apprentice House books or to obtain submission guidelines, please visit www.ApprenticeHouse.com.

Apprentice House
Communication Department
Loyola University Maryland
4501 N. Charles Street
Baltimore, MD 21210
Ph: 410-617-5265 • Fax: 410-617-2198
info@apprenticehouse.com
www.apprenticehouse.com

www.ingramcontent.com/pod-product-compliance
Lightning Source LLC
Chambersburg PA
CBHW070328090426
42733CB00012B/2397